TRUST JESUS

To Bring the Best Out of the Worst

Trust Jesus!
Proverbs 3:5,6
W. E. Berry

TRUST JESUS

To Bring the Best Out of the Worst

William E. Berg

BRONZE BOW  PUBLISHING

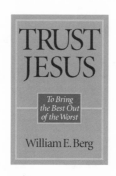

TRUST
JESUS

To Bring
the Best Out
of the Worst

William E. Berg

Published by Bronze Bow Publishing Company
Minneapolis, Minnesota

Printed by Sentinel Printing, St. Cloud, Minnesota

ISBN 0-9715299-5-7

Table of Contents

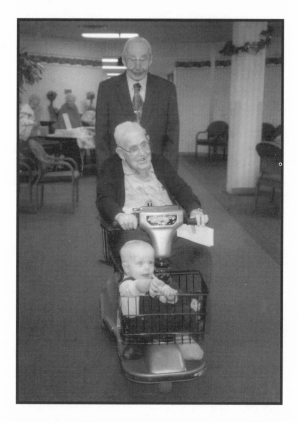

Dr. Conrad giving my great-grandson,
Emery Carlson, age 2, a ride in his
"motorized scooter".

Dedicated to:

DR. THEODORE E. CONRAD

In our nineties, we spent much time together reminiscing, praying, studying the Bible and discussing current issues in Church and society.

Dr. Conrad had a brilliant mind. He had a passion for Eternal Truth as found in the Scriptures. And for Jesus, the Way, the Truth and the Life. His fruitful ministries included the following: College Professor of Greek and Christianity, Academic Dean, Seminary Professor, Counselor to Students, world traveler and research scholar in Bible lands. Yet he was one of the most humble persons I have ever met. He always acknowledged himself as a sinner saved by Amazing Grace. He often spoke of his baptism, never as automatic salvation as many in the Church do, but as a miracle of Divine Grace by which he was chosen to be a child of God.

In frequent visits to his room I would find him in creative activities, reading, working cryptoquip puzzles, listening to great music and working at his computer. Even at the age of 100 he was typing and running on his printer Amnesty letters to be sent to the violators of human rights on behalf of victims being tortured in many countries.

As chairperson of a senior group in my apartment center, I scheduled Dr. Conrad to open each fall program with a message. He gave a series of messages under the general topic, "Behold That Which is Lowly", such as "Behold the Lowly Ice Cube", "Behold the Lowly Hard-boiled Egg", "Behold the Lowly Crib". Out of these titles came powerful and challenging messages.

Dr. Conrad specialized in gems of insight. Some examples follow:

Don't be afraid to be unabashedly Christian.

To be a good teacher, you need always to be a fellow learner.

In teaching or in preaching, it isn't enough to just talk. Until they get it, you haven't said it.

Never trust a theologian; always check his words. You can trust Jesus! He is God's Cosmic Act of Grace.

Alice didn't have terminal cancer. She had transitional cancer — transitional from life to Life. So I don't grieve; I believe.

Some of his favorite verses from the book of Colossians follow:

"Christ, our life."
Colossians 3:4 (His ordination class motto.)

"When Christ, who is our life appears,
then you also will appear with him in glory."
Colossians 3:4 (Blessed Assurance!)

"He (the Christ) is before all things,
and in him all things hold together."
Colossians 1:17.

Even at the age of 100, Dr. Conrad was keeping in touch with his 6 children, 20 grandchildren and 49 great grandchildren. He used the telephone daily to keep in touch with his family, greeting them on their birthdays.

Each day as I count my many blessings, I include partners like Dr. Conrad, who have given me such a big lift on my life journey. He would be uncomfortable about all the good things said about him in this dedication, but I know he would lay all tributes at the feet of Jesus. I also know that he would say "Amen" to the message of this book and especially to the teachings of Jesus upon which the message is based. I know that he would prefer the title of this section to be, "Dedicated to the Glory of God."

Dr. Conrad often spoke longingly of his desire to be together with his beloved life partner, Alice, in heaven. Together we looked forward to the great reunion with loved ones, and to the best, seeing Jesus our Saviour face-to-face.

Dr. Conrad died on December 29, 2005 at the age of 100.

PREFACE

In Ecclesiastes 12:12 we read these words:

"Of making many books there is no end. . ."

Go into any book store, religious or secular, and there we can find a deluge of information, inspiration, challenge, drama and the arts, and books of fiction. There are books that demean and destroy persons. There are books that poison mind and spirit. We also find biographies of noble persons and great books from great minds. There are books of true inspiration and beauty that nurture mind and soul. We can tell much about a person's character and values by what he or she reads and keeps in a personal library.

In recent years, among the many categories of words and books, "self-help" has perhaps surpassed them all. With checklists, numbered "easy steps" and individualized will power, self-help literature proposes that we can help ourselves out of our problems with determination and renewed self-reliance.

At this point in history we find ourselves in just such a place. I predict that a deluge of books and writings will go into the minds of readers following disruption and devastation in the lives of millions of persons caused by hurricanes and other natural disasters that seem so prevalent in our headlines of late. When we try to describe these disasters in words, we need to come to terms with the fact that we are trying to "express the inexpressible" and "describe the indescribable". How true it is that when the dikes of human ideas fail, the torrents of words start flowing.

Commentators, with their reports and images, cannot possibly paint a real picture of the terror and tragedy. A city under terrorist attack. Cities sinking in infected waters with dead bodies floating by. Thousands of persons who have lost all possessions huddled together in stadiums and auditoriums without sanitation, water and food, watching persons in their midst die. Persons on roof tops screaming for help and rescue. Nor can commentators convey the hopeful answer to such devastation. Valiant rescuers transporting lives to safety, one by one or in groups. People from every state in the Union ready to help, together with rescue operations coming from many other countries.

Who can picture all of this in words? I cannot comprehend with my thoughts and words the incomprehensible. I did not have to endure the agony and the suffering of these tragedies. Oh yes, I care, I cried, I contributed money and I prayed, but truly understanding such events is beyond me, beyond all of us, even those who suffer.

So why am I writing a book? I write because these stories of our day, significant and tragic though they are, do not represent the full story. For amidst all of these current stories remains the ever-unfolding story of God around us and within us, bringing the help, hope and healing we all need.

At the very center of human history we see the intervention of Jesus who entered into the suffering of the world. He suffered more than any person has suffered in the history of the universe. In fact, He endured indescribable pain and agony in the greatest rescue operation our world has ever seen.

> *"But he was wounded for our transgressions,*
> *he was bruised for our iniquities;*
> *upon him was the chastisement that made us whole,*
> *and with his stripes we are healed."*
> ISAIAH 53:5

We learn of Jesus' ability to bring the best out of the worst first from God's Word, but I have also found it to be true throughout my own life experiences. I call this the "gift of firsthandedness".

Most recently for me are the lessons I gained as a result of my own illness. On March 2, 2005, at the age of 94, I suddenly collapsed in my apartment. My strength was completely drained. That night marked the beginning of a long battle with pneumonia and its effects on the human body. Following hospitalization and time spent in a rehabilitation center, it took several months for me to recover enough strength to continue in ministry.

Perhaps the word "worst" is not the most accurate way to describe my illness. However, in terms of my age and the long process of recovery, I hope that my experience will reveal how our Lord uses these "interruptions" and sometimes heavy burdens to bring great blessings into our lives.

My Lord brought so many blessings out of both the experience of severe illness and recovery, I can testify that it is hard to tell which is the greatest blessing. Here are some of the lessons I learned:

1. In the rehabilitation process I learned that with prayer and rehab specialists sent by our Lord, you can do the impossible; you can do what you can't!

2. Complete dependence upon others can be a very special gift from God. It is the human drama of our ultimate dependence upon Him. The journey from independence to interdependence and then to dependence can help lead us toward maturity.

3. During each day, I spent many hours in meditation and prayer, intercession and praise. It became clear to me that it is easy to become so busy in service to our Lord that we neglect the "daily quiet time" and God's special place of renewal for us. God's program of rehabilitation for mind and spirit took precedence over other exercises.

4. I learned first hand how long and tedious sleepless nights can be for my many friends who have told me of this malady. Dr. Theodore Conrad, my cherished friend and mentor, taught me what I call the "ABC's of Divine Medication for Sleeplessness". In this exercise of mind and spirit, I would try to recall a Bible verse beginning with each letter of the alphabet from A to Z. For example, "*All have sinned and come short of the glory of God.*" — Romans 3:23. "*Behold, the Lamb of God, who takes away the sin of the world.*" — John 1:29. It was a helpful exercise except for the frustration of missing three or four letters. A similar exercise was used for the first lines of hymns.

5. I learned that being a resident in a care center brings special opportunities to witness for Jesus. My caregivers included those of the Christian faith (Catholic and Protestant), Hindu, Muslim and

other religions. Only our Lord knows how effective or ineffective my witness was. Missing opportunities to witness for my Lord and Saviour, and often giving a weak testimony of His love for all persons, have often burdened and convicted me. It is easy to say, "God loves you, God bless you," but it requires divine grace and guidance to speak of Jesus in a loving and non-judgmental way. It is important that our lives confirm our Christian faith.

I did have the advantage of referring to my books which were on the table. Persons of all faiths seemed to be interested in them. These books, which helped in my ministry there, are as follows:

Show Me the Way to Go Home — Journey to the Promised Land
A *Strange Thing Happened to Me on the Way to*
    Retirement — I Never Arrived
It's Okay Not to be Okay — IF
Jesus — Final Authority on Marriage and Same-Sex Unions

6. I know that my Lord used loving and self-giving family members in an indispensable way in my healing. Each morning I call the role of my family, mentioning each one by name. Their daily visits helped me more than medication, exercises or any other treatment. They came to visit from near and far. While I am grateful for my family, each day I pray for lonely persons who are without immediate family.

7. I learned to be more grateful than ever to my Lord for my Church. My pastors came to both the hospital and rehabilitation center to share the life-giving body and blood of my Lord and Saviour in Holy Communion. Friends sent cards beyond my count telling of their prayers for me. I know that the Christian Church today is suffering from schism and confusion caused by varying interpretations of God's Holy Word. God grant that the Holy Spirit and Jesus will open the scriptures to us, giving us minds to understand and obey! However, I thank God for the Church. E. Stanley Jones, missionary and evangelist, wrote in one of his books, "The Church has many critics but no rivals in the work of human redemption." So often I have witnessed and experienced this truth, but my recent illness brought fresh gratitude for this work of God's divine grace in the world.

8. Several times a week I go with my walker three blocks from my apartment to the Augustana Care Center to visit friends. I can now relate more effectively to the residents there. I should add that the persons I visit are ministers to me, God's special gifts to me. Even in the persons who no longer recognize me, I see Jesus' mighty works in their past lives, and I am inspired and lifted. How true it is that there is no retirement policy in the Kingdom of God, either for healthy or afflicted persons!

During months of convalescence, inevitably the question presses itself upon my mind, "Why was my life spared and why am I still here?" It has become clear to me that one reason is to write this book, even at the age of 95. Here again I want to share the anguish and concern I feel in my spirit for those who have had to suffer far more pain and discomfort than I shall ever have to experience. In comparison to the pain of losing all earthly possessions, the indescribable grief of seeing loved ones dying on every side and watching the fury of nature demolish homes and hopes, my illness fades into a gentle impact on my body. Yet this illness and other experiences which have come into my life have shown me that if I trust in Jesus, He will bring something good and many blessings out of the difficulties we encounter in life.

It may sound easy for me to say, "Hang in there!" to someone going through tough times. I recall a story that is related to this "hang in there" greeting. It is the story of a father who was reading his paper in the living room. Suddenly, he heard his young son upstairs shouting over and over again, "Hang in there, hang in there, you will make it, you will make it, hang in there!" Knowing that his son was upstairs alone, he went to investigate. He found his son bending over a book, repeating the same words, "Hang in there!" Asked for an explanation, the son said, "Well, Dad, I was reading about my hero in this book. He was having an awful time. I felt so sorry for him. Then I turned to the last chapter of this book. I found there that my hero came out just fine. But he didn't know this. So I have to come back to him and keep on telling him to hang in there, everything will be okay."

We may not have the luxury of knowing how the details will all work out, but we can know the final chapter for ourselves. Traveling with the One who walked the way of suffering before us, we can watch Him transform suffering into a song of hope. He can turn burdens into blessings. He can make pain redemptive and purposeful. He can replace fear with faith. He can give us a new and reassuring view of death, dying and the process of dying. Because of Jesus we **do** know how the story comes out. So we can "hang in there" with hope.

In our struggles we wonder, "Is there more to dying than death?" Oh for a thousand tongues to shout, "Yes!" We can hear, not a shout, but a quiet, intensely personal and eloquent "yes" from a beautiful daughter, wife, mother and friend who helped bring assurance and hope to many in need in the midst of her own suffering. Our daughter, Marcia, died at the age of 52, in the prime of her self-giving ministries. Six months before she died, she wrote these words,

> "Though my experience with cancer has not changed my daily routine much, it certainly has affected my thoughts and feelings about life. Things I previously took for granted — like getting up in the morning and being able to go to work or even something as mundane as going to the grocery store — I now see these as things to be thankful for. Each new day is a gift to be appreciated. I have been deeply touched by the love, support, and prayers of family and friends — a blessing beyond measure.

> "Above all else, I have experienced the reality of God's faithfulness. I have realized that life holds no guarantees for any of us and that the only constant, the only certainty I can hold on to is His love and care, come what may. I am so thankful for this faith in a personal, ever-present God, a faith that has been nurtured through the years and that now has become such a source of peace and strength."

Many promises in the Bible assure us that our Lord will not only sustain us in difficult times, but He will bring the best out of the worst. This was Marcia's experience.

"My grace is sufficient for you,
for my power is made perfect in weakness."
2 CORINTHIANS 12:9

"And call upon me in the day of trouble;
I will deliver you, and you shall glorify me."
PSALM 50:15

"God is our refuge and strength,
a very present help in trouble."
PSALM 46:1

"For I know the plans I have for you," says the Lord,
"plans for welfare and not for evil,
to give you a future and a hope."
JEREMIAH 29:11

But as the title of this book suggests, trust, specifically **trusting Jesus**, is key to receiving the hope that these promises hold for us. The following illustration will help us remember this word.

Brennan Manning in his book, *Ruthless Trust*, tells of the brilliant ethicist, John Kavanaugh, and his visit to "The House of the Dying" in Calcutta, India. On the first morning there he met Mother Teresa. She asked, "What can I do for you?" Kavanaugh asked her to pray for him. "What do you want me to pray for?" she asked him. He voiced the request that he had borne thousands of miles from the United States. "Pray that I have clarity." She said firmly, "No, I will not do that." When he asked her why, she said, "Clarity is the last thing you are clinging to and must let go of." When Kavanaugh commented that she "always seemed to have the clarity he longed for", she laughed and said, "I have never had clarity; but I have always had His trust. So I will pray that you trust God."

In the dictionary, the word "trust" is defined as "belief, confidence in the honesty, integrity, reliability and justice of another person or thing." God, in His holy Word, reminds us to trust Him:

"When he calls to me, I will answer him;
I will be with him in trouble, I will rescue him and honor him.
With long life I will satisfy him, and show him my salvation."
PSALM 91:15,16

"Trust in the Lord with all your heart,
and lean not on your own understanding.
In all your ways acknowledge him,
and he shall direct your paths."
PROVERBS 3:5,6 (NKJV)

In the writing of this book, the question comes to my mind, "Why write now, in the midst of flux and uncertainties?" I can only answer that now is the time for me to write for two reasons.

First, I have the advantage of being 95 years old. This gives me the gift and blessing of **perspective** from my Lord. I was a child in the midst of the deep depression years in our country. I lived through the influenza epidemic of 1918, two world wars, the cold war, the Korean War, the war in Vietnam and other wars. I have learned what wars can do and what they cannot do. I have learned what we can do with an atomic bomb and the dangers of living in an atomic age. I have visited some of the most poverty-stricken places in the world, such as Haiti, many parts of India and Palestine. I have served two inner city parishes where I learned the meaning of "the Church without walls", and that the Church exists to bring the message of hope and reconciliation to those outside its fellowship.

It is true, as someone has said, that wisdom comes with age and sometimes age comes all by itself. My protection against age without wisdom is not found in books created by human minds. It is found in Jesus and His Word in Luke 24:45:

"Then he opened their minds to understand the scriptures."

My prayer as I write is found in Psalm 51:6:

"Behold, thou desirest truth in the inward being;
therefore teach me wisdom in my secret heart."

My second and most important compulsion to write is in response to the promise of my Lord in answer to my fervent prayers for guidance found in Psalm 32:8:

> *"I will instruct you and teach you the way you should go;*
> *I will counsel you with my eye upon you."*

The greatest gift I have from my Lord as I begin writing this book is a **"Biblical perspective"**. Looking at the world through eyes enlightened by eternal truth gives us another view of life. My life partner of 55 years, my wife Marta who is now in Heaven, wrote a book of narrative verse entitled, *Seen and Unseen*. In her poem, "Skepticism", we find a prayer for this gift:

> "An acorn
> fell on her head,
> and Henny Penny ran around shouting,
> 'The sky is falling down.'
>
> Each friend she met joined her
> and the dread news became
> FACT.
>
> Around and around they went
> until they met Foxy-Loxy.
> He swallowed up the news
> and the newsmakers.
>
> Let me never join
> a Henny Penny parade.
>
> Give me the gift of skepticism
> about all the words that are spoken,
> and all the words that are written.
> Let me test them
> in the crucible of
> common sense,
> history's lessons,
> and, above all,
> Eternal truth."

And so it is with the promise of God's guidance and with the gift of His perspective that we seek answers to some of the disturbing questions of our time:

Where is God when disasters take place?

If Jesus is my friend, why doesn't He take me out of my suffering?

If not Jesus, who do we believe can bring the best out of the worst?

Were those who are affected by tragedies any worse sinners than those of us who continue to live in comfort zones?

How do we move past the "worst" in our lives? Do we settle for the good that we can do rather than for the "best" that God can do?

How does God come into our lives and make His "best" possible for us in every circumstance?

As we seek, we will soon realize that not only are these the questions of our time; they indeed represent the questions of all time. We will discover that Jesus has answered these questions with His eternal truth.

"If you continue in my word, you are truly my disciples, and you will know the truth, and the truth will make you free."
JOHN 8:31B,32

"Who shall separate us from the love of Christ? Shall tribulation, or distress, or persecution, or famine, or nakedness, or peril, or sword?. . . No, in all these things we are more than conquerors through him who loved us. For I am sure that neither death, nor life, nor angels, nor principalities, nor things present, nor things to come, nor powers, nor height, nor depth, nor anything else in all creation, will be able to separate us from the love of God in Christ Jesus our Lord."
ROMANS 8:35, 37-39

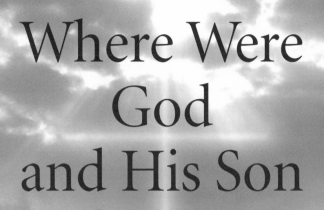

Where Were God and His Son

Chapter One

WHERE WERE GOD AND HIS SON?

As I was writing this chapter I received shocking news. The headline in the Minneapolis, Minnesota morning paper told of the October 9, 2005 earthquake in Pakistan. In that article with its gruesome details, the estimate of fatalities was 18,000. Since that time the estimates have grown to 89,000. Pictures of men and women digging frantically with shovels and with their hands in the rubble, trying to find and rescue loved ones staggers the imagination. The human spirit cries out in indescribable grief, sorrow and concern. It is estimated that more than half of the casualties are children. Who can assess the sorrow and pain of parents in this tragic loss of their children? Suffering in the aftermath of the disaster is heartbreaking. Victims are living in flimsy tents in freezing weather, without hope.

In a partial list of major earthquakes we find the stories of thousands lost. In 1556 an earthquake in China took 830,000 lives. In 1923 there were 143,000 fatalities in an earthquake in Japan. In 1948, 110,000 persons perished in an earthquake in Russia. Joining the list of deadliest earthquakes is Indonesia where in 2004, 283,000 persons died.

More recently, hurricanes and a tsunami have left us awash in grief and disbelief as we have witnessed massive loss of life, loss of home and loss of basic human necessities within the fury of nature. In the wake of disasters such as the "Katrina" and "Rita" hurricanes in 2005, the question, sometimes shouted in anger, sometimes in despair and hopelessness, was often heard, "Where are the local, state and federal government rescue teams?"

Hurricanes. Floods. Earthquakes. September 11th. Terrorist attacks around the world. One tragedy after another comes and with each core-shaking experience returns the instinctive human question in the face of suffering, "Where is God?"

After the 9/11 terrorist attacks in New York and Washington, the initial response was shock and disbelief that it could happen, followed by a frenzy of fear. However, rising beyond the fear came the massive rescue efforts that inspired the world. Then something even more significant happened. In the aftermath of 9/11, millions instinctively started to call upon God for help. The President of the United States called for a day of prayer. Churches were crowded with worshipers, praying for help and guidance from Almighty God. Those of Muslim, Buddhist, Hindu and other religions were calling upon their gods. Indeed, our God was in the midst of the terror and tragedy as we felt our most profound need for Him.

In a sermon entitled, "The Supremacy of Christ in an Age of Terror", John Piper reminds us of the presence of God and His Son:

"So even in our own experience — in our own souls — believers and unbelievers, there is a kind of witness that the world of evil and pain and misery and death is not a meaningless place. It is not a place without a good and purposeful God. Some people — not all — have found in the greatest evil — the time of greatest sorrow — the greatest need for God and the greatest evidence of God.

"It happens like this. A great evil happens — say the holocaust with 6,000,000 murders. Or the Stalinist Soviet gulag with many more than that sent to their deaths. In the midst of these horrors, the human soul, that had been blithely pursuing its worldly pleasure with scarcely a thought about God and with no serious belief in any absolutes like evil and good, or right and wrong — happily living in the dream-world of relativism — suddenly is confronted with an evil so horrible and so great as to make the soul scream out with ultimate moral indignation: No! This is wrong! This is evil!

"And for the first time in their life they hear themselves speaking with absolute conviction. They have a conviction of absolute reality. They know now beyond the shadow of a doubt that such a thing as evil exists. They admit that all their life up till then was a game. And now they are confronted with the stark question: If there is such a thing as absolute evil — if there is a moral reality that is above and different from the mere physical process of evolutionary

3

energy plus time plus matter — then where does it come from and what is it based on?

"And many people discover in this moment of greatest evil that there is only one satisfactory answer: There is a God above the universe who sets the standards of good and evil and writes them on the human heart. They are not purposeless chemical reactions in our brains. They have reality outside of us, above us, in God. Paradoxically, therefore, the times of greatest human evil have often proved for many to be the times when God is most needed and most self-evidently real. Without him evil and good are simply different electrochemical impulses in the brain of mammal primates called Homo sapiens. We know — you know — that is not true."

As Pastor Piper explains, crises in the world and in the specific experiences of our own lives lead us intuitively to questions of faith. In these moments it is important to understand that the central question of our faith is not, "What do you believe?" but rather, "Whom do you trust?" The title and emphasis of this book bring readers deeper into the direct, challenging and sometimes disturbing question, "Do you trust God and His Son, Jesus?"

To answer this question we must study the life and teaching of Jesus. Who is this Jesus and what did He live for? On His way to the Cross to die for His enemies who scourged Him, for His friends who deserted Him, and for your sins and mine, what was Jesus doing?

E. Stanley Jones in his book, *Is the Kingdom of God Realism?*, can help us with the answer. He gives an eloquent testimony to the realism of Jesus and His kingdom:

"He laid aside His carpenter's tools one day and went into the little synagogue at Nazareth. There He announced His manifesto of good news to the poor — the economically disinherited; release to the captive — the socially and politically disinherited; the opening of the eyes of the blind — the physically disinherited; the setting at liberty them that are bruised — the morally and spiritually disinherited and the proclaiming of God's year of Jubilee — a fresh world beginning. Here was spirituality ('the Spirit of the Lord is upon me') functioning as redemption to the economic, to the social and political, to the physical, to the moral and spiritual, to the collective. The whole of life was to be faced realistically and redeemed. He ended by saying, 'Today this scripture has been fulfilled in your ears' — the Manifesto had been fulfilled in Himself, the Manifesto and the Man were one, the Program and the Person had come together. When He thus joined the two, He made it realism, and not idealism."

In another book, *The Christ of the Indian Road*, E. Stanley Jones writes:

"He did not discourse on the dignity of labor — He worked at a carpenter's bench and His hands were hard with the toil of making yokes and plows, and this forever makes the toil of the hands honorable.

"As He came among men He did not try to prove the existence of God — He brought Him. He lived in God, and men looking upon His face could not find it within themselves to doubt God.

"He did not paint in glowing colors the beauties of friendship and the need for human sympathy — He wept at the grave of His friend.

"He did not teach in the schoolroom manner the necessity of humility — He girded Himself with a towel and knelt down and washed His disciples' feet.

"He did not discourse on the equal worth of personality — He went to the poor and outcast and ate with them.

"He did not prove how pain and sorrow in the universe could be compatible with the love of God — He took on Himself at the cross everything that spoke against the love of God, and through that pain and tragedy and sin showed the very love of God.

"He greatly felt the pressing necessity of the physical needs of the people around Him, but He did not merely speak in their behalf — He fed five thousand people with five loaves and two fishes.

"He did not merely tell us that death need have no terror for us — He rose from the dead, and lo, the tomb now glows with light.

"Many teachers of the world have tried to explain everything — they have changed little or nothing. Jesus explained little and changed everything.

"Many philosophers speculate on how evil entered the world — Jesus presents himself as the way by which it shall leave."

As we study the life of Jesus, we find that God, in His Son, has offered the ultimate answer to our cry for help: they were there. God and His Son were there suffering and dying with the thousands of victims.

One man discovered this truth for himself. He was sitting on the bus reading his Bible. The man sitting next to him said, "Are you reading about God in that book?" The man replied, "Yes, I am." Then came another question, "Are you reading about that good God of yours?" Again came the answer, "Yes." With bitterness in his voice he shared another question, "Where was that good God of yours when my boy died in the war?" Came the quiet reply, "I think He was watching His own son die."

Indeed, God, in His Son, was there in each of the tragedies of our day and beyond. He is ever-present in the suffering of every human heart. We can trust this Jesus, who not only brings the best out of the worst, but who is Himself our best hope in the midst of our confused and struggling human race. He offers us an eternal hope.

The Psalmist observes this inescapable presence of God-with-us in Psalm 139:7-12 where we read:

> "Where can I go from your spirit? Or where can I flee from your presence? If I ascend into heaven, you are there; if I make my bed in Sheol, you are there. If I take

the wings of the morning and settle in the farthest limits of the sea, even there thy hand shall lead me, and thy right hand shall hold me fast. If I say, 'Surely darkness shall cover me, and the light around me become night,' even the darkness is not dark to thee; the night is as bright as the day, for darkness is as light to thee."

Would that we would all experience to a greater depth the truth of the presence of God. He is there!

The story is told of a mother who was lying awake at night during an electrical storm, worried and anxious about problems in her life. Her daughter in the next room was awakened by the thunder and cried for her mother. Her mother lay down beside the little girl who went right to sleep. But the mother stayed awake with her continuing anxious thoughts. Again, thunder awakened the little girl who cried for her mother. Her mother did not say a word; she just touched the hand of her child. The little girl said, "Oh Mother, I forgot you were here," and she went right to sleep. Then the mother prayed, "Oh Lord, please forgive me. I forgot You were here," and she went right to sleep. In the midst of the many storms, tragedies and natural disasters, we can be sure that God was there. Jesus was there. And they are here!

In the chapters that follow, we will together experience His presence and explore why we can trust Jesus in times of trouble, how He is present even in our darkest moments and how the presence of Jesus can transform the worst into the best. We begin this journey together in the light of God's promise:

"Fear not, for I am with you, be not dismayed, for I am your God;
I will strengthen you, I will help you,
I will uphold you with my victorious right hand."
ISAIAH 41:10

Chapter One
STUDY GUIDE

*This Study Guide may be used for
personal meditation or group discussion.*

1. The title of this chapter asks a very personal question that often surfaces in the face of a crisis: "Where were God and His Son?" Have you ever found yourself asking this question of faith? Take a moment to reflect on that time. What was it like to experience the seeming absence of God during such a time in your life?

2. How did your faith change or grow as a result of wrestling with this question of God's presence? Did you ultimately find Him to be present in your own crisis? If so, how? If not, where do you think He might have been, looking back now?

3. Who or what did God use in your life to remind you of His divine presence with you during your difficult time? How can you share this hope that you received with others?

4. How does your faith in Jesus lead you to trust Him and His plans for you, whatever your circumstances?

Rescue—
A Drama

Chapter
Two

RESCUE — A DRAMA

The title of this book is not *How to Bring the Best Out of the Worst*, but rather, *Trust Jesus to Bring the Best Out of the Worst*. Why can we trust Jesus, beyond anything or anyone else, to bring the best out of the worst? The answer is found by taking a long look at the cross. Here we see the Son of God, Creator of the Universe, in whom all things were made and before whom every knee in heaven and earth shall bow, dying a torturous and ignominious death on the cross. He died there to make possible the forgiveness of our sins by a holy God. He died there a completely innocent man, accused by those who hated Him and sentenced to death by a cowardly and shameless governor. Here we see the most tragic event in all human history, and yet we also hear the best news this world has ever heard or ever will hear. It is the only news that carries us beyond suffering, the good news of redemption and new life for all who believe.

Divine Revelation affirms to us the way Jesus brings the best out of the worst. We read in Psalm 40:2-3:

> *"He drew me up from the desolate pit, out of the miry bog, and set my feet upon a rock, making my steps secure. He put a new song in my mouth, a song of praise to our God. Many will see and fear, and put their trust in the Lord."*

I recall reading the story of a three-year-old child who fell down a narrow shaft which was being dug for a well. It is difficult to even imagine the fear and fright in this child 20 feet below the surface in complete blackness, unable to move arms or legs. It seems that the entire nation was a witness to the rescue attempts. They brought in heavy machinery to dig a parallel hole and then to tunnel to the place where the child was trapped. The celebration and joy of the huge crowd when the child was brought to the surface was beyond description.

I read of another spectacular rescue of a child in which a man went down into the hole head-first with arms stretched down and with his feet tied to a rope at the surface. The rescue was successful. We have read of miners trapped a mile or more beneath the surface and of the heroic rescue operations. We have prayed for the families of miners who died in the explosions. In this chapter we note that rescue operations require more than reassuring words. Decisive action is needed, whether in the tragedies in the world or in the crises of suffering and loss in our own lives. Jesus said in John 12:32:

> *"and I, when I am lifted up from the earth,*
> *will draw all men to myself."*

Come with me to the scene of another rescue, a Divine rescue. It is the dramatic story of a God who personally executed the greatest rescue operation in the history of the universe.

The drama begins with a person in a pit, sinking in the mire of sin and despair. Many panaceas are set forth for purposes of rescue from pain, suffering and the effects of sin. But the trouble with all of them, as we will see, is that they do not work. Their adherents specialize in delivery of words, but never in the deliverance of persons.

Let us look at a processional of would-be rescuers stopping at the edge of the pit.

First, a man comes to the edge of the pit, stops and gives a learned discourse on "The Polarization of Resources for Purposes of Self-Projection". Not being able to get a rise out of the man in the pit, he lectures again on the subject, "The Self-Expressive Life of Freedom from Restraint". Finally, he ends with this oratorical flourish, "When you come to the end of your rope, tie a knot and hang on." Then he throws down a rope — both ends. This represents *sterile intellectualism*. There is no lifting power here. It is both irrational and irrelevant. The trapped person remains in the pit.

Another man comes by and speaks eloquently on "The Art of Thinking". He says, "Reason your way out. Think it through; use your head." This is *rationalism*. And the trapped person thinks and sinks.

"Lift yourself up by your own bootstraps," declares another

would-be rescuer. He does not even provide the bootstraps. This is *humanism*. The person in the pit strains and stretches and sinks deeper.

Next, several intelligent-looking individuals come along. They are solid citizens who love to do good. They hold a committee meeting at the edge of the pit. They elect officers — president, vice president, secretary, treasurer, and even a chairperson in charge of doing good. They have a long business meeting. There are endless discussions and some arguments. They get the life-history of the sinking man (all the while desperate cries are heard from the pit); they get impressive statistics and then make copies of their report — duplicate, triplicate and quadruplicate, which they will carefully file away. Finally, with much fanfare and satisfaction, they decide to feed the person in the pit, to clothe him, and to make him as comfortable as possible in the pit. This is *humanitarianism* without the quality of redemptive and divine concern that can help set people free to live more abundantly.

Next comes a promoter with a smooth line. He moves the person, but not out of the pit. He says, "Just sign here on the dotted line and join my organization, and you will be free." This is *institutionalism*. The person in the pit joins eagerly and is still stuck.

Several young people come along. They sing ribald songs at the edge of the pit and tell shady stories. When this fails to help, they decide to put on a party in which the liquor flows freely and is generously shared with the person in the pit. In their drunken stupor, several jump down into the pit. This is *hedonism*. Life is lived at a low level. Persons have no inherent worth. There is no rescue, only ruin.

"That is not mud down there," says another spectator. "It's all in your imagination. Get mud out of your mind and you will be free." The poor person in the pit thinks clean thoughts. As he seeks to concentrate on things that are lovely and pure, the mud presses and clings and pulls him deeper. This is *agnosticism*. It belittles truth and scoffs at the idea that sin can hurt you or that you need the lifting power of a cross in order to be free.

One man stops at the edge of the pit and says in mournful accents, "There have always been people in pits. There will always be people in pits, and there is nothing you can do about people in pits because people were made to dwell in pits." This is *nihilism*, the philosophy of despair.

A leader in a prominent church, a philanthropist who often rises to speak on the golden rule and on the fatherhood of God and the unity of all people, comes along and says quickly, "What color is the skin of this person? Is he white or black? I can't see. What is his nationality? We must move slowly here and not do anything rash. We must be careful not to help the wrong person." It is hard to find a word that describes this philosophy; perhaps *fascism* in one of its subtle forms. And humanity sinks deeper as this man speaks eloquently about unity to his all-white listeners.

Two active church members, on their way to a prayer meeting, take a fleeting look at the man in the pit. One says, "We cannot stop now. This would make us late for our prayer meeting. But we will be sure to pray for you." This is *Pharisaism*. Meetings are substituted for person-to-person ministry. Prayer is substituted for obedience.

Then Jesus comes. He always comes to the place of human need. Our Saviour not only reaches down. He leaps down into the mire. He makes no speeches. ***He is the message.*** And the message reaches the person! Jesus, the Son of God, Creator of the ends of the earth, King of Kings and Lord of Lords, in whom all things were made and by whom all things cohere — Jesus sinks into the mire of human sin and guilt. With unspeakable tenderness, yet with amazing power, He lifts the sinking person out of the mud and gets him up and out to the edge of the pit. He calls from the bottom of the pit, "You are free. Go and sin no more." Then He sinks in the mire of our sin, transgression and demonic rebellion against a holy God. He dies to make us free. This is *Christianity*.

> *"Consequently he is able for all time to save those who draw near to God through him, since he always lives to make intercession for them."*
> HEBREWS 7:25

13

In the procession of irresponsible and irrational persons that preceded the real rescue, not one seemed to be aware of the extreme need of the man in the pit. If we have a superficial view of sin, suffering and evil, we will surely come with ridiculous and impractical suggestions for help and rescue.

The suffering and tragedy that we encounter in this world may defy adequate explanation but do have a common source. We live in a fallen world. When sin, the deliberate rejection of God and His moral law, first entered the picture, the world and all humanity experienced a cosmic separation from the best that God had intended in creation. The result of this fallenness, created by a sin-wrecked humanity that is separated from its Creator, is the pit into which sinners have fallen. Jesus is the only rescuer who can lift us to safety and new life. The vertical bar of His cross of torture and shame reaches from the heart of God to the bottom of the pit. The horizontal cross-bar tells eloquently of His loving arms ready to lift whoever will call upon Him for help.

The Rescue Drama tells us how Jesus rescues us fallen sinners. Jesus, King of Kings, Lord of the nations, Lord of history, was a side-by-side sufferer. He took upon Himself our helplessness and hopelessness in the fearful darkness of our lives. Indeed, Jesus alone brings God's ultimate and original best out of the worst in our lives and world.

However, when we are unwilling to face the truth about our depravity and about the destructive nature of sin and a fallen world, we minimize the need for this Divine Rescue. We fumble our way toward eternal death amidst feeble and futile efforts to save ourselves or others. If we convince ourselves that we are never truly lost, that our sin is not too serious, we will never need a Saviour. As surely as we minimize sin and our need for saving, we will tone down the gospel message. How long will it take us to learn that a denatured gospel can never capture and convert a depraved humanity? A superficial view of sin always means a superficial acceptance of the gospel. Such acceptance is rejection in one of its most tragic forms. A superficial view of suffering in the world costs us the awareness of the power of God at work in our lives.

It seems that in our day most people sense little need to be saved from sin and judgment. They strive to be saved from many ills but not from that which is most deadly and destructive. In fact, it would appear at times that the most flaming "evangelists" of our day are the perpetrators of television and radio commercials. In one sense they offer "salvation" to all who will listen, believe and buy. The intent of what they say could be interpreted thus, "Buy and be saved." Saved from what? From headaches, heartburn and colds. From all kinds of mysterious germs. From perspiration perils and from romance that fades. Using hidden persuaders and psychological devices, and in accents of great urgency, they offer salvation from discomfort and inconvenience, from drudgery and dishwater hands. Buy and be saved from tooth decay, from filtered-out flavor and from insecurity that only a bank account and credit card can cure!

Are these the ills and dangers from which we need to seek rescue above all others? It would seem so from the actions, attitudes and stewardship practices of many persons. Others maintain that terrorism is the greatest evil. Some cry, "Save us from atomic incineration, from a nuclear holocaust, from fallout, from depression, from a forced surrender of the American way of life, from those who would snatch our freedom." Indeed, these are real perils.

However, persons who have intellectual as well as moral and spiritual integrity see symptoms of deep-seated ills of the spirit that defy our power or ingenuity to heal. What are some of these ills from which we need to be saved? Perversion, irrationalism, demonic rebellion against a Holy God. From our lostness and estrangement, pride and pretense, prosperity that desensitizes us to the suffering and pain of others. From self-sufficiency, superficial faith, nominalism. From a form of godliness without power, human striving and spiritual exhaustion. From a crooked and perverse generation, from being too well-adjusted to the evils of racial inequality, the crippling effects of discrimination and the madness of militarism. From a doctrine of justification of sin without justification of the sinner. From sin-sickness which is unto eternal death. From

15

the devil, the world and our own flesh. From the wrath and judgment of a just and holy God.

In the world's greatest rescue operation, bringing persons out of their worst to His best, there is a question that should persist in our minds. **Saved — For What?** For adding years to our lives or life to our years? For rebuilding cities and lives? The Bible gives the answer:

> *"By this we know love, that he laid down his life for us;*
> *and we ought to lay down our lives for the brethren."*
> I JOHN 3:16

I recall the story of a drowning man who was calling for help. The lifeguard reached him, brought him to shore and revived him with CPR. When he could speak the man said to his rescuer, "Sir, how can I ever thank you for saving my life?" The lifeguard replied, "You can show your gratitude by showing to the world that your life was worth saving."

Jesus specializes in the rebuilding of lives and the restoration of hope. The words of the hymn, "My Hope is Built on Nothing Less", remind us:

"His oath, his covenant, his blood
Sustain me in the raging flood;
When all supports are washed away,
He then is all my hope and stay.

Refrain: "On Christ, the solid rock, I stand;
    All other ground is sinking sand,
    All other ground is sinking sand."

Regardless of the calamities of our lives, Jesus remains our Hope and Stay, our Divine Rescuer, our trustworthy Deliverer. He believes that we sinners are worth saving and offers power to bring new life and hope to others in His name.

Chapter Two
STUDY GUIDE

*This Study Guide may be used for
personal meditation or group discussion.*

1. Imagine that you are the person in the pit described in this chapter. Describe your personal "pit". What is it that is entrapping you or has entrapped you in the past?

2. What or who did you find around you that promised to "rescue" you but could not?

3. How did God execute His rescue operation in your own life in this situation? What did you have to do in order to cooperate and allow yourself to be rescued?

4. Divine Rescue is not reserved for major crises alone; God wants to redeem us from all of the pitfalls, large and small, in our lives. Walk through the five steps of Divine Rescue found in Psalm 40:2-3:

   He lifts. . .
   He sets my feet upon the rock. . .
   He guards my steps. . .
   He gives me a song of praise. . .
   Others will be blessed by my song. . .

5. Where in your life **now** is God waiting to implement this plan for your best?

FROM EARTHQUAKES AND FLOODS TO HOPE

Chapter Three

FROM EARTHQUAKES AND FLOODS TO HOPE

It can be overwhelming to consider the cost, not only of homes and belongings, but especially the vast cost of human life lost in recent earthquakes and floods. Through television and technology we have all shared in the experiences of those most affected by recent natural disasters. Suddenly, even events that are far away geographically come into our living rooms and classrooms, causing the world's story to become personal and present in our lives.

Of the many commentaries and reports issued during and after such events, it is interesting to note that historians seldom mention two of the most significant earthquakes of all time. Bible scholars and persons of the Christian faith should be acquainted with them. In these earthquakes we read, not of huge and tragic death tolls, but of life and hope – life out of death and hope of eternal life.

In the previous chapter the truth of God's rescue of us in our lostness and sin was dramatized. In this chapter we will examine how God brought the best out of the worst through what happened to Jesus during two earthquakes. We will also see what happened during a flood. It did not contaminate lives and property. Rather it offered cleansing from the poison of sin. In these larger-than-life events we find hope for a suffering world and the promise of salvation and eternal life.

Matthew is the only one of the four gospel writers to tell about these earthquakes. The first one happened 2000 years ago on a hillside outside the walls of Jerusalem. Jesus Christ, Son of God, Creator of the universe was hanging on a cross. In his own body and spirit all the sins of all people since the beginning of the human race were placed by a just and holy God. These sins include the sins of terrorists, murderers, rapists, torturers, all evil in the world and yes, all your sins and failures and mine.

This event is recorded in Matthew 27:45-54:

> *"Now from the sixth hour there was darkness over all*
> *the land until the ninth hour. And about the ninth hour*

Jesus cried with a loud voice, 'Eli, Eli, lama sabach-thani?' that is, 'My God, my God, why hast thou forsaken me?' And some of the bystanders hearing it said, 'This man is calling Elijah.' And one of them at once ran and took a sponge, filled it with vinegar, and put it on a reed, and gave it to him to drink. But the others said, 'Wait, let us see whether Elijah will come to save him.' And Jesus cried again with a loud voice and yielded up his spirit. And behold, the curtain of the temple was torn in two, from top to bottom; and the earth shook, and the rocks were split; the tombs also were opened, and many bodies of the saints who had fallen asleep were raised, and coming out of the tombs after his resurrection they went into the holy city and appeared to many. When the centurion and those who were with him, keeping watch over Jesus, saw the earthquake and what took place, they were filled with awe, and said, 'Truly this was the Son of God.'"

Indeed the earth shook on that day. What happened in that earthquake? In that earthquake outside of Jerusalem, we find that the best this world has ever known came out of its worst suffering and tragedy. There was darkness over all the land at midday. The temple veil was ripped from top to bottom. There was now free access to the holy presence of God, which before had been hidden behind the veil to everyone except the high priest who could go in there once a year to seek atonement for sinners. The curtain dividing priests and worshipers, Jews and Gentiles, bound and free was torn apart.

In his death and resurrection Jesus destroyed the power of death. The tomb lost its power, the grave lost its terror and death lost its tragedy. Here again we see that Jesus brought life out of death, the best out of the worst.

In the midst of His terrifying torment on the cross, Jesus cried out in agony of body and spirit, "My God, my God, why have you forsaken me?" Even worse than the physical agony was the pain of being separated from his Heavenly Father. Nothing worse, absolutely nothing worse could happen to Jesus.

In his book *My Utmost for His Highest*, Oswald Chambers wrote:

> "The Cross is the point where God and sinful man merge with a crash and the way of life is opened — but the crash is on the heart of God. . .Never build your preaching of forgiveness on the fact that God is our father and He will forgive us because He loves us. It is untrue to Jesus Christ's revelation of God; it makes the Cross unnecessary, and the Redemption "much ado about nothing". If God does forgive sin, it is because of the death of Christ. God could forgive men in no other way than by the death of His son, and Jesus is exalted to be Saviour because of His death. 'We see Jesus... because of the suffering of death, crowned with glory and honor.' The greatest note of triumph that ever happened in the ears of a startled universe was that sounded on the cross of Christ — 'It is finished'. This is the last word in the Redemption of man."

Jesus, the Son of God, wore the crown of thorns in order that we may wear the crown of divine glory and grace which shall never fade.

The dirty spikes of man's hatred pierced the holy hands and feet of Jesus so that His hands could be stretched out to us, offering His love and grace, and that with His feet He would walk with us all the way to Heaven.

The dirty spittle of our demonic hatred marred His holy face in order that your face and mine may be radiant with an eternal hope.

Jesus wore the robe of ridicule to make it possible for us to wear the robe of righteousness that will cover all our sins as we stand before a holy God on judgment day.

He cried, "My God, my God, why have you forsaken me?" in order that we may never have to walk alone in this dangerous world.

The earth trembled at the sight of God's Son giving His life for yours and mine, as Death itself was put to death. Yet, as powerful and monumental as this earthquake was on that Good Friday, there was another earthquake just three days later that would forever alter the definition of "hope."

> *"Now after the Sabbath, toward the dawn of the first day of the week, Mary Magdalene and the other Mary went to see the sepulchre. And behold, there was a great earthquake; for an angel of the Lord descended from heaven and came and rolled back the stone, and sat upon it. His appearance was like lightening, and his raiment white as snow. And for fear of him the guards trembled and became like dead men."*
> MATTHEW 28:1-4

We have already reviewed in this book the death toll of several destructive earthquakes in history, but the earthquake described here by Matthew reports no deaths. Rather than causing death, new life was revealed and death was proven conquered.

> *"O death, where is thy victory? O death, where is thy sting? The sting of death is sin, and the power of sin is the law. But thanks be to God, who gives us the victory through our Lord Jesus Christ."*
> I CORINTHIANS 15:55-57

The earthquakes of our day inevitably cause severe loss — loss of life, loss of homes and property, loss of valued family treasures, loss of livelihood. But the earthquake on Resurrection morning brought only gain.

> *"But whatever gain I had, I counted as loss for the sake of Christ. Indeed I count everything as loss because of the surpassing worth of knowing Christ Jesus my Lord. . ."*
> PHILIPPIANS 3:7,8

Included in the best that Jesus brings out of the worst are what we shall call **The Divine Corrections**, the ways in which Jesus makes right what sin had made wrong in the sight of God. A partial list follows:

THE CORRECTION OF RELIGIOUS LEADERS

In the earthquake following Jesus' death on the cross, the high priest, Scribes and Pharisees, enemies of Jesus, though unnerved by the upheavals in nature, must have had a sense of satisfaction about "their mission accomplished". They thought they had eliminated Jesus who exposed their hypocrisy and threatened their power. However, their actions only magnified the wonder of the power and glory of God. In the process of trying to destroy Jesus, they destroyed themselves and their right to be trusted as religious leaders.

In his book, *The Word Became Flesh*, E. Stanley Jones tells how the enemies of Jesus tried to get rid of him:

"How far can evil go in a world of this kind? How far can force go? How far can lies and clever manipulation go? How far can you cover up the designs of evil in the cloak of good and religion? The answer is that evil can go a long, long way—it can put the Son of God, the Creator of creation, on a wooden cross—wood which He created. That's a long, long way. How far can force go? It can nail the Creator's hands upon the cross. And it can lift it up for all men to see what force can do. How far can lies and clever manipulation go? It can twist the truth of Him who was the Truth and make it into a falsehood and can thus crucify Him on misquotations. How far can evil designs be wrapped in the cloak of religion and good? It can go a long way—it can make evil seem good—they crucified Jesus in the name of God, His Father. They made it appear that they were protecting the sacred name of God. 'You have heard the blasphemy!' they cried. Evil, force, lies, perverted religion can go a long way in a world of this kind.

"They can do these things today and tomorrow, but the third day? No! For Jesus gathers all these questions in His body and answers them in His resurrected body and spirit the third day!"

THE CORRECTION OF POLITICAL OPPRESSION

At the time of the Good Friday earthquake it appeared that the power of an oppressive government had prevailed, and that political intrigue worked well in the attempt to get rid of Jesus. However, let us note from the resurrection story in Matthew's gospel that following the earthquake an angel came and removed the stone from Jesus' tomb. The soldiers guarding the tomb found Him already gone and they trembled and became as dead men. The rolled-away stone revealed that Jesus had within himself final authority; not even death, much less the power of the Roman army, could hold him. (Matthew 28:2-4).

THE CORRECTION OF THE VIEW OF WOMEN

There was another very significant correction that took place on the morning of the earthquake and the removal of the stone from Jesus' tomb. It was the correction of the view of women in society and in the Church. In Mark 16 we read that it was the women who first discovered that Jesus was not there. In John 20 we find that Mary Magdalene was the first person to whom Jesus revealed Himself in His resurrection body. She was the first one to bring the good news to the disciples as she announced, "I have seen the Lord!" Peter and John came to the tomb, found it empty and left.

It was Mary who first told the greatest news the world has ever heard — a woman who, in the society of that day, could not enter fully into the worship of the temple. Jesus called her by name. Mary Magdalene and the other women who stayed at the cross to watch Jesus die and who came early on the Sabbath to the sepulcher were not ordinary women of their day. They were followers of Jesus. They were highly honored by their Creator God, not as second class citizens but as first bearers of His resurrection good news. Unlike the society in which He lived, Jesus affirmed that women were also made in the image of God as told in the Genesis story. It could be said that Jesus was the founder of the Women's Liberation Movement!

Because of Jesus' attitude toward the role of women, we are encouraged to think of women in history as truly great leaders, pioneers, professionals, volunteers, missionaries, teachers, front-line workers, people of vision and courage. Above all, we think of the honor surpassed by none, their calling to be mothers and preservers of the Christian family without which society cannot prosper. Indeed, women have been used mightily by God to bring the best out of the worst.

THE CORRECTION OF THE POWER OF SIN AND DEATH

Greater than any other correction issued by that Easter earthquake was the divine correction of the power of sin and death. Because of Jesus, funeral services were turned into Resurrection services. In memorial services, surely tears will flow freely in the midst of deep grief and suffering. However, now these can be celebrations of hope and joy and praise in memory of the loved one and friend who was released from suffering and pain in this fallen world and who is forever with the Lord and Saviour in Paradise Regained. Jesus said in John 14:2,3:

> *"In my Father's house are many rooms; if it were not so, would I have told you that I go to prepare a place for you? And when I go and prepare a place for you, I will come again and will take you to myself, that where I am you may be also."*

I should add, incidentally, that there is an unfortunate trend in the Church today in memorial services. The focus is often on the good deeds and merits of the departed person. In speaking in positive terms about him or her, it should always be remembered that if there is anything good in any of us, it is the goodness of the crucified and risen Saviour and His righteousness.

I believe that memorial services are one of the greatest missionary and evangelistic opportunities for the Church. In the audience there are often persons who never worship the living God and have no time for Him in their busy schedules that center on their own personal interests. Persons will be present of other religions or of no religion to honor the deceased. And so it is here, at the place of death, that we should honor Christ who forever gives life and hope to the world.

One of my favorite stories is about a ten-year-old boy. His name was Elmer. There were nine other boys in his Sunday School class. Elmer was under-developed both mentally and physically. Sometimes his classmates were impatient with his slowness. On Easter Sunday morning their Sunday School teacher gave each boy a small box. He said, "I want you to go out to the churchyard and find something that reminds you of the meaning of Easter. Put it in the box. Come back in 15 minutes to show what you found. We will vote on the first prize winner." Returning with their boxes each one told about the contents. One boy had a flower in his box. He spoke of the beauty of Easter. Another boy had blades of green grass. He told of new life in springtime. The next boy had a stone in his box. He told about the stone that was rolled away from the tomb. One by one they reported. At last, they came to Elmer. He opened his box and it was empty. Before he could explain the other boys "lit into him" with criticism and disgust. They said, "Elmer, can't you do anything right? You were supposed to put something in your box." Elmer started to cry. Then he said, "Well, I didn't want anything in my box. I wanted it to be empty. It reminds me of the empty tomb. Jesus wasn't there. He was alive." The boys were very quiet and then voted for Elmer as first prize winner. Several months later Elmer died. During his memorial service nine boys marched up the center aisle and placed nine empty boxes on Elmer's casket. The teacher told the story of Elmer's box. Elmer, though dead, was still speaking. "The tomb is empty. Jesus is not there. He is alive." There was another message for many that day. "Elmer is alive. His afflicted body is in the casket, but his spirit is with Jesus in Heaven."

> "Blessed be the God and Father of our Lord Jesus Christ! By his great mercy we have been born anew to a living hope through the resurrection of Jesus Christ from the dead, and to an inheritance which is imperishable, undefiled, and unfading, kept in heaven for you."
>
> I PETER 1:3,4

How true it is that the earthquakes on Calvary's hill and at the tomb of Jesus restore to the life of every believer a living hope!

Thus far in this chapter we have written of two earthquakes in the Bible. As indicated in the title of this chapter, we will now consider floods. We remember the floods which followed the disastrous hurricanes, Katrina and Rita. Pictures of the suffering and devastation still overwhelm us.

But the flood that I will now describe will not be remembered as a flood by most persons. I can only testify that, for me, this flood has meant not danger, loss or pain, but my survival and new life and hope in the midst of death and dying. We read of the origin of this flood in John 19:33,34, telling what the Roman soldiers did immediately after they saw that Jesus had died:

"But when they came to Jesus and saw that He was already dead, they did not break his legs. But one of the soldiers pierced his side with a spear, and at once there came out blood and water."

This is the **flood** of the cleansing blood of Jesus, flowing across the entire world to rescue, cleanse and save. Jesus' blood, mingled with water, reminds me of the water of my baptism. The water and the blood. The water and the Word. The saving **flood** indeed!

In I John 1:7c we read these words:

" . . .and the blood of Jesus His Son cleanses us from all sin."

Two incidents from my own life illustrate for me the wonder and the saving power of the healing streams flowing from Calvary's mountain.

In 1936 I was serving my seminary internship in a large church in Chicago. A member of the congregation became ill and urgently needed a blood transfusion. My blood was the right type. In those days there were no blood banks. I lay on a bed beside my friend who was on the operating table. Blood flowed from my body directly into hers. Her health was restored. Several weeks later, she knelt at the altar of the church. There she heard the words of our Lord, "My body broken for you, my blood shed for you." She was healed by blood for her body and by the blood of the Son of God for her body and spirit. This is total healing —- wholeness.

Years later, on a Christian Ashram tour (a spiritual retreat), I was in Benares, India. We were in a boat on the Ganges River. It was a high and holy day on which faithful pilgrims came from many places far and near to submerge themselves in the Ganges River, there to be cleansed and prepared for higher destiny in their after-death lives. Men and women were not only submerging themselves in the polluted waters of the river, but they were swallowing the water to be made clean on the inside. It was a tragic sight but so familiar in that we all seek to make ourselves clean when all the while our attempts to cleanse only make us more polluted, inside and out. On the shore we saw a dead person in a beautiful silken shroud lying on the funeral pyre. Holy Ganges water was sprinkled upon her and then her body was destroyed in the flames.

I still remember the song that we sang at our Christian Ashram worship service that Sunday morning, a song that meant more to me than ever before:

"There is a fountain filled with blood,
Drawn from Immanuel's veins,
And sinners plunged beneath that flood
Lose all their guilty stains,
Lose all their guilty stains."

There is indeed a healing stream that flows from the body of our crucified Saviour. May we pray the prayer of a well-loved hymn:

"Jesus keep me near the cross,
There a precious fountain,
Free to all, a healing stream,
Flows from Calv'ry's mountain.
In the cross, in the cross
Be my glory ever,
Till my raptured soul shall find
Rest beyond the river."

It is important to remember that it was not only a healing stream of blood that flowed from Jesus' body; it was the greatest **flood of unconditional love** that this world has ever known.

If we truly believe, we will accept God's power to use these Good Friday and Easter earthquakes and the Calvary flood, not only to help us survive but to bring rich blessings to us. And we will receive power to be part of our Lord's rescue operation to bring light and hope in a dark and dangerous world.

Let us move from fear and lament to praise as Jeremiah did in Lamentations 3:21-23:

> *"But this I call to mind, and therefore I have hope:*
> *The steadfast love of the Lord never ceases,*
> *his mercies never come to an end;*
> *they are new every morning; great is thy faithfulness."*

Let us keep our eyes on the Cross where the very best came out of the very worst. Then we will keep singing the song of hope and praise to Jesus. It is the song that never dies!

Chapter Three
STUDY GUIDE

*This Study Guide may be used for
personal meditation or group discussion.*

1. Tragic earthquakes and natural disasters are destructive, but as we have noted, often great things have risen out of the devastation. Have you had an experience in your life that initially seemed devastating but later proved to be the painful opening of the way to tremendous blessing? How has God already used the worst to unveil some of the best in your life?

2. In this chapter, we review some of the Divine Corrections that the Cross of Jesus initiated in the world and society. Are these corrections still relevant today? Do you feel these corrections are important as a follower of Jesus? Why or why not?

3. How might God be inviting you to participate in His ongoing work of redemption in the world within any one of these areas of Divine Correction?

JOURNEY FROM THE WORST TO THE BEST

Chapter Four

JOURNEY FROM THE WORST TO THE BEST

In the last chapter we learned that we can move from disasters in nature and in our lives to divine hope found in Jesus. In this chapter we face a practical and pressing question — how do we make this move? How do we move from the "worst" to the "best" on a day to day basis? Even if we believe that such a journey is possible by faith, what are the steps toward that end? What is the process that can carry us closer, not only to a better situation, but ultimately to God's eternal best for us? These are the questions we will explore together in this chapter.

With such practical questions in mind we can be grateful to our God, who in His divine holiness took on human flesh, doing more than simply telling us how to live but also demonstrating for us the way to live. He not only saves us from the "worst"; He walks through it with us. Therefore, it is no surprise that God's Word is filled with examples of very human people living very human lives, all on a journey toward (or away from) God's best. Let's take our own journey back through a few of these stories to see what we can learn from them.

The first stop on our journey is recorded in the book of Genesis, chapters 37 and 39-45. This is the story of Joseph, who was sold by his jealous brothers into slavery and taken to Egypt where he was ultimately sold to Potiphar, an officer of Pharaoh. This man made him overseer of his house and all that he had. When Potiphar's wife tempted Joseph saying "lie with me", Joseph steadfastly refused. She became so angry that she falsely accused Joseph of attacking her, resulting in Joseph's imprisonment. There Joseph met Pharaoh's butler and baker whose dreams God enabled him to interpret. Two years after their release from prison, Pharaoh had a dream which none of his magicians or wisemen could interpret. His butler then told Pharaoh about Joseph who could interpret dreams.

When Joseph told the king that his dream meant that there would be seven years of plenty followed by seven years of famine in Egypt, Pharaoh was so impressed that he took his signet ring from his hand and put it on Joseph's hand, setting him in authority over all the land of Egypt. During the seven years of famine people came from all over the world to Joseph, who filled their orders for food while he filled the Egyptian treasury with money.

Joseph's brothers, the same ones who had earlier sold him into slavery, also came down from Canaan to Egypt to buy food during the famine. During several visits, Joseph, still unrecognized by his brothers, gave severe orders to his brothers to test them. These visits end with a dramatic climax as Joseph finally reveals himself to be the brother they had betrayed. He then brought his father, Jacob, his brothers and their families to Egypt where they lived and prospered.

The following story tells what happened following Jacob's death. It is recorded in Genesis 50:15-20:

> "When Joseph's brothers saw that their father was dead, they said, 'It may be that Joseph will hate us and pay us back for all the evil which we did to him.' So they sent a message to Joseph, saying, 'Your father gave this command before he died, 'Say to Joseph, Forgive, I pray you the transgressions of your brothers and their sin, because they did evil to you. And now, we pray you, forgive the transgression of the servants of the God of your father.' Joseph wept when they spoke to him. His brothers also came and fell down before him, and said, 'Behold, we are your servants'. But Joseph said to them, 'Fear not, for am I in the place of God? As for you, **you meant evil against me; but God meant it for good,** to bring it about that many people should be kept alive, as they are today.'"

Indeed, God brings good out of evil and the best out of the worst! By faith Joseph saw God at work in the midst of his suffering. Out of what appeared to be the worst for Joseph came the best, not only for him but also for his family and for an entire country. This divine plan was good for Joseph and it is good for us.

Another story in our journey from the worst to the best is recorded in Luke 15. We are taken to a far country where a son is spending his inheritance in riotous living. Penniless and starving he gets a job feeding swine. Finding him in this situation we read in Luke15:17 these significant words, *"But when he came to himself"*. This was the crisis point in his journey from the worst to the best. He did not blame others for his tragic downfall. He did not say, "My father was too strict" or "My big brother bugged me" or "My fair-weather friends deserted me" or "That stingy farmer wouldn't give me any-thing to eat". Rather, his words indicate that he knew that he had made a mess out of his life and that he was guilty and needed to make a confession to his father.

This was the moment of the great exchange for the son, leaving the pig pen for a welcoming party in his father's home. The picture of his father, who had been watching every day for his son's return, running down the road to meet him, is indeed one of the most beautiful pictures in the Bible. When they meet he does not reproach his son and remind him that he has disgraced himself and his family. Rather, he provides a robe to cover his son's filthy rags, new shoes for his feet and the ring of sonship on his finger. He arranges for a grand homecoming celebration.

This story is popularly known as "The parable of the prodigal son". I have another title for it, "The story of the unconditional love of the father for his two sons, one lost in the far country and one lost at home".

It is an eloquent story indeed about God bringing the best out of the worst. As the prodigal son "came to himself", he realized and accepted the truth of his own sin; there was confession in his heart and in his words. This return to the truth of his wrongs, rather than choosing blame or further running, enabled him to return to the truth that was even larger than his wrong; the truth of his father's unconditional love for him. The elder son had remained at home, attempting to earn or demand his father's respect. In his destructive bitterness he missed the greater truth of his father's love. Consequently, he squandered both the relationship and the blessing of celebration. There are many lessons for all of us here as we make our way from the worst to God's best.

We continue our biblical journey from the worst to the best with a story that begins in Genesis and continues through to Resurrection morning.

It was the worst of times when our first parents were to be banished from the Garden of Eden and the ploughshare drawn over paradise. We cannot sin against a holy God and get by. But it was also the best of times in terms of the divine announcement as God spoke to the tempter, Satan, saying:

> *"I will put enmity between you and the woman,*
> *and between your seed and her seed;*
> *he shall bruise your head, and you shall bruise his heel."*
> GENESIS 3:15

It was the worst of times when flood waters covered the earth and all living souls perished, except for eight persons, the family of Noah. But it was the best of times as we see a huge boat riding the crest, a place of refuge from death. (Genesis 7:21-23)

It was the worst of times when the angel of death stalked the land of Egypt, killing the firstborn in every Egyptian home. There was wailing and weeping. But it was the best of times as we see blood on the doorposts of the Israelite homes and everyone safe on the inside. (Exodus 12:21-23)

It was the worst of times when the rebellious Israelites were dying on every hand, bitten by poisonous snakes. But lift up your eyes. It was also the best of times. There was a bronze serpent on a pole. Each person who looked at it was healed. (Numbers 21:6-9)

It was the worst of times some 2000 years ago when Israel was under the cruel oppression of the Roman government and under the ruthless tyranny of King Herod. But we hear the cry of a newborn baby in a manger in Bethlehem. It was also the best of times. Unto you is born a Saviour!

> *"And the angel said to them, 'Be not afraid; for behold,*
> *I bring good news of a great joy which will come to all the people;*
> *for to you is born this day in the city of David a Savior,*
> *who is Christ the Lord.'"*
> LUKE 2:10,11

It was the worst of all times on a hill outside the Holy City. There, the very people Jesus loved and came to rescue and save, held him in derision and nailed him to a cross of agony and torment. It was earth's darkest hour. The sun hid its face for shame. They and all of us sinners tried to get rid of goodness and God. But here again we find the best of times!

"But he was wounded for our transgressions,
he was bruised for our iniquities; upon him was the chastisement
that made us whole, and with his stripes we are healed.
All we like sheep have gone astray;
we have turned every one to his own way;
and the Lord has laid on him the iniquity of us all."
ISAIAH 53:5,6.

It was the worst of times for the disciples and followers of Jesus when their Lord was killed. Their hopes died with Him. But it was the best of times on that first Easter morning when the tomb was empty and Jesus came out alive to be with them forever!

"But the angel said to the women, 'Do not be afraid;
for I know that you seek Jesus who was crucified.
He is not here; for he has risen, as he said.
Come, see the place where he lay.'"
MATTHEW 28:5,6

This is the Jesus of whom I am writing in this book. He alone can bring the best out of the worst for all who place their trust in Him. It is reassuring to know that the darkness and the tragedies of this world magnify the light that Jesus brings.

"Again Jesus spoke to them, saying, 'I am the light of the world;
he who follows me will not walk in darkness,
but will have the light of life."
JOHN 8:12

Without the realities of the cross and the resurrection of Jesus, it would be impossible to believe or see that the best could come out of the worst. Jesus is our supreme example of this possibility and the hope of our own journey toward God's best.

If we go beyond the stories recorded in scripture and if we search the experiences of our own lives, we can see that God brings the best and the greatest blessings for us out of some of the most difficult events. By reviewing some of the tragedies and disasters throughout history, we can note how "hope springs eternal" through the work of God in the world and in our own hearts.

Our first stop is New York City. We remember 9/11, the terrorist attacks on the World Trade Center in New York and the Pentagon in Washington, D.C. I recall that I cried out aloud when I saw pictures of those twin towers crumbling to the ground with thousands of helpless victims going to their deaths. But we recall that this place of tragedy was transformed into a place of prayer. Our president set aside one day as a National Day of Prayer. Prayer not only changes things and changes our perspective, it also changes us and keeps us looking up to see where our help comes from. Millions of people not only looked down at the rubble and the bodies, they also looked up to our God who was indeed suffering in the midst of the disaster and who gives new hope in the midst of the great tragedies of life. We also recall the army of rescuers. They looked down and saw the dying amidst the burning rubble and risked their lives in one of the greatest rescue operations in history. So we look up as we are reminded to do in Psalm 121:1,2:

"I lift up my eyes to the hills. From whence does my help come?
My help comes from the Lord, who made heaven and earth."

Our next stop is Oklahoma City. We recall the bombing of a building which took 168 lives. Visiting the Oklahoma City memorial was one of the most sobering times in my life. Among the many tourists there one heard very little conversation. We walked around in an atmosphere of reverence out of respect for the victims. Seeing those 168 vacant chairs of the Memorial would rule out light-hearted banter. When I saw the special walls dedicated to the children, and the inscriptions and pictures and words drawn by children, it was a time for tears. When I crossed the street from the Memorial, I saw the most impressive sight of all. The Catholic Church had erected a large statue of Jesus on the lawn. I shall never forget seeing that eloquent tear coming down His face.

Our next visit is to the city of Hiroshima in Japan. There I participated in a memorial service with the pastor of a church that had been destroyed by the atomic bomb. Many church members had perished, but out of the ashes and the devastation had risen a beautiful new church building under the cross. This was one of the most moving moments of my life. When I was asked to speak and pray at that memorial gathering, I could tell of the power of the cross in the lives of those who perished and in the lives of us who were gathered there. I prayed, "God have mercy on the tens of thousands still dying slowly as victims of the bomb. Lord have mercy upon Japan. Lord have mercy on the United States of America. Lord have mercy on your Church. And Lord, may this never happen again as we follow your way, the way of the cross".

The world needs to remember this tragedy and eliminate the stockpiles of nuclear weapons, just a few of which could destroy the entire world.

But even in this atomic age and the "worst" moments it has already provided, we can find traces of God's best at work. I recall the story of twelve Japanese girls whose faces were so marred by the bomb that they could never appear in public. They were taken to the United States for plastic surgery. One of the girls had twelve operations and still her face was far from cleared and healed. She had spent many months in a Christian home where she had met Jesus, her friend and Saviour. Before the thirteenth operation she said to the doctor, "Please do not feel bad that you cannot give me a new face. You see I've got a new heart and I'm all okay!" We praise God for medical science and for healing through surgery. Above all we praise Him for transformation of lives and for healing of the spirit.

As we believe in God's power to bring the best out of the worst and find hope for ourselves, we must also carry this hope to others. This is a vital part of the journey to which we all are called. We are called to carry forth God's hope into the world not only through our prayer, which is a good beginning, but also through action. It is through the call of God and the model of Jesus that we, His followers, should also enter into the suffering of the world as He did, embodying His presence of hope and peace that only He can give in the midst of turmoil. And this call goes out to all of us who would follow Christ, regardless of age or station in life.

Continue our journey with me to a meeting room in the apartment center where I live. An Amnesty International group session is in progress. Members of the group range from 70 to 100 years of age. Dr. Ted Conrad is reading three letters to be sent to leaders of three countries and to their ambassadors in Washington, D.C., protesting specific acts of torture. Dr. Conrad, age 100, types and runs 95 copies of letters which members of the group then personally sign and send to those involved in the torture. (Since this was written, Dr. Conrad went to be with his Lord and Saviour.)

In a recent meeting, we heard of a pregnant woman who was suffering torture for conceiving a child in violation of China's family practice policies. Following a forced abortion she spent 18 months in prison. There, among other tortures, she was suspended from the ceiling and severely beaten.

Surely the "worst" includes this kind of torture, so rampant in many countries. We send letters to officials of the USA protesting torture of prisoners in Iraq and other places.

But out of this "worst" come concern and intervention for the victims. Leaders are urged to prosecute those who torture and to work for justice in tangible ways. And more. This woman in China, with Amnesty officials on the scene, knows that someone cares and is working for her release. Think also of the joy that comes to members of our group as we care and pray and work for justice for suffering persons all over the world. In using our voices for justice we are granted the grace of a purpose larger than ourselves. We rejoice when we receive word of favorable responses to our letters, and this spurs us on to continue in practical as well as financial support of Amnesty International.

For one final stop on our journey from the worst to the best, let us go back to the story of a man who found God's best out of his worst situation and whose words have since encouraged and inspired many during their worst moments. We now stop in the middle of the Atlantic Ocean. H.G. Spafford was on his way to England following the Chicago fire. He had sent his wife and children to England during the rebuilding of his business. Their ship went down during a mid-Atlantic storm. The mother survived but their four children drowned. On his way to meet his wife, as they were passing the place of the disaster in the mid-Atlantic, he wrote his famous hymn, "When Peace Like a River Attendeth My Way". We recall two stanzas of this hymn:

"When peace, like a river, attendeth my way;
When sorrows, like sea billows, roll;
Whatever my lot, thou hast taught me to say,
It is well, it is well with my soul.

Though Satan should buffet, though trials should come,
Let this blest assurance control,
That Christ hath regarded my helpless estate
And hath shed his own blood for my soul."

Surely the Lord brings the best out of the worst. With H. G. Spafford we too can be certain of this and find rest. The record of scripture and even the records of our own lives tell us over and over again: the recurring theme of the love of God is inherent in His world. My wife, Marta, expressed certainty in God's provision of the best from the worst in her poem entitled "Surely" from her book, *Seen and Unseen*:

"Surely goodness and mercy
shall follow me. . .

There was that word again — surely.

How can anyone say surely in a day of
tumultuous change?

Or had the Psalmist noted

that there is an absolute certainty
in the universe,
that God's law is unfailingly constant?

On the strength of its constancy,
persons can leave Earth and function in space.

The nurtured bud always opens into bloom.
Ice always forms at the freezing point.
Gravity never takes a vacation.

And so it is with God's moral law. . .
Repentance gives birth to joy.
Peace is a partner of trust.
Love opens doors closed by hate.

God's certainties are written into
the very heartbeat of life itself.

Yes, SURELY."

Surely, indeed. We can trust God for the peace that only He can give through Jesus!

"Peace I leave with you; my peace I give to you;
not as the world gives do I give to you.
Let not your hearts be troubled, neither let them be afraid."
JOHN 14:27

Chapter Four
STUDY GUIDE

This Study Guide may be used for
personal meditation or group discussion.

1. This chapter focuses on the journey from the worst to the best, with God as our constant Companion along the way. What are some of the spiritual milestones from your own journey?

2. What did each of these milestones reveal to you about the character of God? How did these experiences impact your relationship with Him?

3. How has God invited you to turn these milestones into ministry? How have you been able to encourage or help others because of the hidden blessing of these experiences? Consider some examples from Scripture:

   Genesis 3:15
   Genesis 7:21-23
   Numbers 21:7-9
   Luke 2:10-11
   Matthew 28:5-6
   Revelation 22:20

4. Take a moment to praise God for His presence with you throughout your journey, especially from the worst to the best.

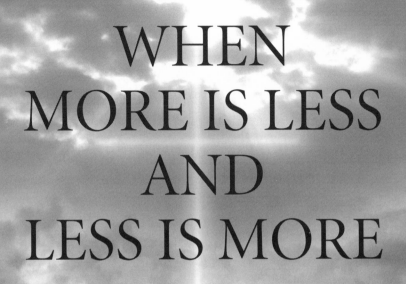

WHEN
MORE IS LESS
AND
LESS IS MORE

*Chapter
Five*

WHEN MORE IS LESS AND LESS IS MORE

As we continue our struggle together to rebuild and restore our world following tragedy after tragedy, the cries for "more" become the common language of the would-be problem solvers. Cries are heard for "more government involvement", "more financial assistance", "more donations", "more working together". Truly, each of these is needed for the future, but it is easy to demand more from others than from ourselves. What is the self-giving Christian response to this situation? Are we also in the crowds demanding "more" from others or are we willing to live with less ourselves so that we can give freely to those in need, all in the name of Jesus? It is a hard question but one which we must answer if we intend to stay on the way with Jesus.

The urge for "more" is a human urge and common in our culture. One of the crises of society today is consumerism. It is the insatiable desire for more — more money, more power, more perks and prestige, more fun and entertainment, more comfort and convenience. This drive for more material goods forces us to work more than we ever have as a society. We spend more. We eat more. We owe more. Today we have more unfulfilled desires and less true joy and satisfaction in life's relationships. Philip Yancey, in an article in *Christianity Today* writes, "The sexual revolution of the 1960's, which promised liberation, has resulted in a soaring divorce rate and epidemics of sexually transmitted diseases. This is liberation?"

This could be called the "More is Better" myth. It leads not only to frustration, but to a colossal waste of gifts and talents that our Lord has given us, not least for self-giving, loving service to others.

MORE approval of sin and LESS power to rescue lost and confused persons.

MORE of "doing what I please" and LESS of "being pleased with what I do".

MORE of personal rights and LESS of the rights of others.

MORE dependence upon military might and LESS security for people and nations

MORE contempt for the Ten Commandments and LESS of the life-giving protection they provide.

MORE of roaming in the vast wasteland of television and LESS of self-esteem and respect for life.

Another "More is Better" myth can be illustrated by an event in our family. I call it "more presents — less presence". For 14 years I traveled extensively in the USA and Canada, conducting evangelism missions in the Lutheran Church. Thus I was away from home for many months each year. My coming home was a special event, especially for my young son, Billy. He would say something like this, "Daddy, I'm so glad to see you. I missed you. What did you bring me?" Then his eyes sparkled as he opened the gifts I had brought. After 10 or 15 minutes, he left all the gifts on the floor and said, "Daddy, will you play football with me?" We played a rough and tumble game. Indoors in the winter the ball went flying through the living room. Billy's mother was very patient and very wise. She shared my discovery that our son was much happier and more secure, even with the bumps, when he had his father playing with him on the floor than when he was opening gifts from his father. I share a postscript for the story. Someone asked a father who was playing a rough game with his son, "Aren't you afraid that you will sprain your back?" He replied, "I would rather have a backache today than a heartache tomorrow."

It is true for us as well. We often ask for "things" but it is "presence" that we crave. It is easy indeed to expect and ask for gifts from our Heavenly Father. However, we need to worship Him, not only as giver, but as our Father-Creator in whom we know Jesus, our Saviour. Grace is found, not only in the gifts of forgiveness, new life and hope, but in worship and adoration in His Divine Presence. So we affirm the words of King David in Psalm 16:11:

"Thou dost show me the path of life; in thy presence there is fullness of joy, in thy right hand are pleasures for evermore."

For further study of the "More is Better" myth and resulting crisis afflicting so many in our world today, we present six lessons.

Lesson One — Roots of the Crisis

I quote here illuminating thoughts from Katherine Krause, a writer and poet and a senior editor of this book:

> "We see the roots of this crisis all the way back in Eden with our first father and mother, Adam and Eve. With them, we too have inherited the temptation of the sneaking suspicion that God somehow is holding out on us. When tragedies strike, this suspicion becomes a consuming demand pointed toward the Divine. Rather than living where we are, we stare at the forbidden fruit — whatever it may be in your life or in mine — and we risk everything for just a little "more" of the something that we believe will fix everything or at least get us by.
>
> "But it never does. Never does the drive to consume become sated on its own. We do not have the capacity to satisfy ourselves. As Adam and Eve discovered, giving into this drive only exiles us from our homeland, the place where we belong. Saint Augustine said long ago, 'Our hearts are restless until we rest in Thee.' There is always an echo of something missing inside of our souls until at last we find ultimate peace and then lasting contentment."

Lesson Two — Source of Peace and Contentment

Katherine continues:

> "Where is true peace and contentment to be found, especially in times of turmoil? As humans, we tend consciously or subconsciously to define 'contentment' as the absence of struggle. It would be nice to consider that we could imagine a world without suffering, without pain, loss and death. There is such a place — it is called Heaven — but we do not live there. Not yet, anyway. As citizens of this world and as followers of Jesus, we are invited to be "realists" in this world,

to be both fully informed of the state of the world and the people around us and full of faith at the same time. This is difficult to do in the face of so many tragedies, so much suffering, so many lives lost. It can be overwhelming. It can seem like too much. Indeed, it is too much for any person.

"And Jesus knew this. Our need to find a way of peace in the midst of calamity was on His mind and was a part of His mission in coming to redeem us. To those who would follow Him then and now, He says:

"Come to me, all who labor and are heavy laden,
and I will give you rest. Take my yoke upon you, and learn from me;
for I am gentle and lowly in heart,
and you will find rest for your souls.
For my yoke is easy, and my burden is light."
MATTHEW 11:28-30"

LESSON THREE — THE SUPER BOWL SUNDAY FOOTBALL GAME

We mortals learn things from strange and startling places and in diverse ways. Hopefully, with discernment, especially spiritual discernment, we can learn something from the Super Bowl Sunday football game held in 2006 in Detroit, Michigan.

We have indeed come a long way in the use and observance of Sunday, a long way from the days when this was a day business enterprises and commerce gave rest and respite to their workers who then found time to play and pray and stay together. I should add that this observance did not liberate us from many problems, social and otherwise, in the generation of which I was a part.

The hundreds of millions of dollars spent on the game and on entertainment and other events seemed to go unnoticed as excess. The spending was encouraged as a way to support the economy. But in the midst of screaming spectators, not only on Super Bowl Sunday but in stadiums on other Sundays, do we hear the cries for help from sick and homeless and hungry persons? Super Bowl Sunday should warn us not to celebrate excess while ignoring the poor.

I am a realist. I know that in the stadium and among the television viewers were countless sincere believers in God, faithful church members who give themselves for their Lord and for persons in need.

I should add that I was addicted to sports in my high school and college years. Golf is now my favorite game. At age 95, I still play an occasional game with the help of a golf cart and strong arms when needed.

Let us now consider how this "more" of the Super Bowl football celebration really becomes less of the good and best our Lord has for us:

MORE secularization of the Lord's day, LESS of the healthy benefits our Creator intended for us on this day.

MORE worship of the god of sports, LESS worship of the true God.

MORE time for events that feed and control the emotions, LESS time for developing mind and spirit.

MORE money spent on a passing spectacle, inane ads, stadiums and salaries, LESS money spent for the education of children and youth, for health insurance, for crime prevention and for protection of the environment.

MORE "media control" of the minds and actions of people, LESS growth of mind and spirit toward maturity.

Jesus said in Matthew 6:33 (NKJ):

"Seek first the kingdom of God and his righteousness,
and all these things will be added to you."
All of God's best!

LESSON FOUR — WHEN MORE IS GOOD

In this indictment of consumerism and the lust for more material things, we need to remember our need for more of the best. Indeed, we need more compassion, more suffering with hurting persons, more growth toward spiritual maturity and more disciplined study of the Bible. Familiar songs from my childhood come to mind, among them these words:

"More love to Thee, O Christ,
More love to Thee;
Hear Thou the prayer I make
On bended knee;
This is my earnest plea,
More love, O Christ to Thee,
More love to Thee;
More love to Thee."

Regarding my need for God's more, I recall the pulpit prayer I often used before beginning the sermon:

"Not I, but Christ whose cross alone can save,
Not I, but Christ, victorious o'er the grave.
In every thought and deed and word,
Less of myself, more of my Lord
Whose name forever be adored.
Not I, not us, but Christ."

In John 3:16 we read about Jesus giving Himself for us. We need also to remember I John 3:16 where we read about giving ourselves for others:

> *"By this we know love, that he laid down his life for us;*
> *and we ought to lay down our lives for the brethren."*

LESSON FIVE — WE LEARN FROM A BIBLE STORY

We come now to the "Less is More" section of this chapter. This concept can be understood only in the light of divine revelation. It is a guiding principle that both believers and unbelievers need to learn. Again we quote Katherine Krause:

> "The Bible gives us many examples of the "Less is More" Kingdom concept. In Matthew 14:15-21 (NIV) we read the story of how Jesus fed the five thousand. Let us revisit this story together:
>
> *"As evening approached, the disciples came to him*

and said, 'This is a remote place, and it's already getting late. Send the crowds away, so they can go to the villages and buy themselves some food.' Jesus replied, 'They do not need to go away. You give them something to eat.' 'We have here only five loaves of bread and two fish,' they answered. 'Bring them here to me,' he said. And he directed the people to sit down on the grass. Taking the five loaves and the two fish and looking up to heaven, he gave thanks and broke the loaves. Then he gave them to the disciples, and the disciples gave them to the people. They all ate and were satisfied, and the disciples picked up twelve basketfuls of broken pieces that were left over. The number of those who ate was about five thousand men, besides women and children."

"The story begins with a crisis. There are thousands of people listening to Jesus that day. They have followed him, eager to learn, all the way out into a desert place and it is getting late. People have been in the sun. No one really planned for this kind of a crowd or for this kind of event. As was becoming common in Jesus' ministry, people just seemed to collect wherever he went. But now there was a reality to contend with. A crowd topping five thousand was in need of care. They needed to eat! Jesus sends his disciples out among the crowd to see what they could find. No one was prepared for this. All they came up with was five small barley loaves of bread and two fishes. That certainly was not enough.

"But into this cry of 'not enough' from his disciples, Jesus speaks his word of plenty. He prays over the food, blessing it, and breaks it for distribution. We read that not only was everyone filled by what was provided, there were leftovers.

"So it can be with us in our times of desperation. There are times in our lives when, in reality, we do not have enough. We will not be able to make things work on our own. But it is precisely into this emptiness that God will speak. And when He speaks we will find more than enough and plenty to share with others. That is how the Kingdom of God is intended to work. We surrender our need to Christ, He gives the supply and all are fed as we share the overflow.

"Sharing stories of God's provision in our lives is a tremendous way to share the 'overflow' of God's promises and provisions. We all need to be reminded and encouraged that less really is more."

LESSON SIX — A LESSON FROM A "LESS IS MORE" LIFE

In the midst of the many cries for "more" and indeed the quiet cries for "more" within our own souls, we must consider the hidden "less" that each "more" would sacrifice. To dramatize this concept we introduce you to a woman who knew well the blessings of "Less is More" during her lifetime. It is the remarkable story of Mary Anne Prell. At the age of 25, Mary Anne, a college graduate and teacher, went to Pakistan as a missionary under the World Mission Prayer League. For three years she served her Lord there, adjusting well to a new culture and fulfilling her teaching ministry. In 1954 she came back to the USA to have some strange physical symptoms checked. The diagnosis was multiple sclerosis. For 40 years, until the time of her death, Mary Anne was unable to walk. She continued living a vibrant life, traveling with us to Christian Ashrams in Jerusalem, Bermuda, India and many other places. But as you hear Mary Anne's story it becomes apparent that her story is God's story. It is the story of amazing and sufficient grace in the face of constant pain and suffering, in spite of loss and difficulty. It is the story of God's better plan for her. It is His story in which less becomes more for Mary Anne. Consider her thoughts, taken from a tract that we co-authored before her death:

Less of My M.S. - More of His Love. It is true that I have M.S. But my M.S. fades into the wonder and glory of His M.S., His Miracle Sign, the sign of His cross and of His healing love. I shall always be grateful for the divine diagnosis that my Saviour gave to me.

Less Walking - More Wheeling. How grateful I am for the invention of the wheel and for my wheelchair! I thank Him for my wheelchair ministry, not now in Pakistan but in Minneapolis and many other places. I recall being in Bermuda at a Christian Ashram. My wheelchair was beginning to be a burden. Something wonderful happened there. I surrendered my wheelchair to my Lord at the altar. It was no longer a hindrance, but a blessed way of letting His joy and power be shown.

Less Mobility - More Spiritual Exercise. Through the years my arms and legs have grown weaker. There is no way that I can exercise them. But physical exercise is vital for health. What shall I do? I shall use my "meta-physical exercise machine!" It renews my spirit. Jesus always taught me new ways to carry on when my arms or legs would become weaker. Thank you for the blessed assurance of your Word. And I thank you, Lord, that someday I am going to walk all over your heaven.

Less Healing - More Wholeness. On many occasions prayers have been offered for the healing of my body. I have been anointed with oil. No healing of my body was manifested. But new hope and encouragement filled my heart. At one Christian Ashram service I was prayed for in my wheelchair. A great peace and joy engulfed me. True, I did not get up and walk away from the altar. I knew in my heart, and the intercessors also knew and believed that this would indeed be possible. Such miracles of physical healing under the direct touch of the Spirit surely do happen. That night my body was not healed **but I was healed.** Frustrations, hurts and questions were left at the altar. I was free! I was made whole! I was made whole by a miracle of divine grace, made whole for continuing ministry. I praise Him for allowing me to have M.S., not least to teach me more about **Amazing Grace.**

Less Legs to Stand On - More of His Word to Stand On. An interesting thing happened to me in a handicap cab. My wheelchair was lifted on and fastened on the floor, but not securely. When the cab started, my wheelchair tipped over, and I sprawled on the floor. The shocked driver got me up. When he asked, "Are you hurt?", I assured him that I was not. Of course I believed this because there is no sensation or feeling or pain with my M.S. The next day it was discovered that my leg was broken. The bone would not heal, and my leg was amputated. Now I have only one leg not to stand on!

But the story of my "standing" continues. Recently, my apartment attendant let me slip out of bed, twisting my foot in the process. My ankle was broken. My one leg is in a cast. Thus, now I have two legs not to stand on. But perhaps I should say that I have no legs to stand on. In the experience of my broken legs, I made an exciting discovery. I do not need legs in order to stand. I can stand on the promises of God.

Less Independence - More Dependence. I am deeply grateful to my family and to the government for the privilege of "independent living". But my independence is limited. I have to depend on attendants who give twenty-four hour care so necessary for M.S. persons. I depend upon my "motorized wheels". I depend upon our Lord's special gift to me, brothers and sisters and their families and many friends. During my nursing home days I longed to be more independent, but my great need was to be more dependent upon God, my Father-Creator, Jesus, my Saviour and Lord, and the Holy Spirit, my Counselor and Guide.

Less of Lament - More of Praise. Lament has indeed been a part of my life. I have experienced many dark days of doubt, despair and spiritual dryness. I do not think that I could survive these "down times" unless, from my "down position", I could look up to Him who is always here and always saying, "Come unto me all you who are weary and heavy-laden, and I will give you rest". It's an exciting journey, this journey from lament to praise, from my sinking down to His lifting me up. Is your lament list and mine longer or shorter than our praise lists?

Less of Myself - More of My Lord. In Christ my Saviour I have a new self, one that I can accept with gratitude and express with joy. In Him, I have my highest identity. For many persons, not least for those of us afflicted with M.S., a devastating problem can be low self-esteem. I need to remember that I am created in the image of God, that I am died for by Jesus, His Son and that I am indwelt by the Holy Spirit. I need to remember that my body is the temple of the Holy Spirit. Jesus thought that I, a big sinner, was worth dying for. Now I can affirm the words of Stanley Jones who said, following a severe paralytic stroke, "I am not a witness impaired, I am a witness empowered."

Mary Anne ends her story with an "Altar Call", a call to every reader to come to the Healer: "He is with you all the way, always ready to turn your **less** into His **more**."

When we say "less of myself" it is important to note that we do not say "none of self". Our Lord and Saviour does not wipe us out, as someone has said. He wipes us clean. Our Lord gives us the precious gift of free will. We can turn our backs on Him and reject His offer of new life and salvation. Or, by the power of the Holy Spirit, we can surrender our lives to Him and be filled with His presence and power. For E. Stanley Jones, founder of the International Christian Ashram, the word "surrender" is a key word in the Christian faith. He wrote in one of his books, "In self-realization you try to realize yourself, for all the answers are in you. In self-surrender you surrender yourself to Jesus Christ, for all the answers are in Him".

I close this chapter with the greatest "Less is More" story ever told. It is found in the Bible and is told by Saint Paul in Philippians 2:5-11.

> *"Have this mind among yourselves, which you have in Christ Jesus, who, though he was in the form of God, did not count equality with God a thing to be grasped, but emptied himself, taking the form of a servant, being born in the likeness of men. And being found in human form he humbled himself and became obedient unto death, even death on a cross. Therefore God has highly exalted him and bestowed on him the name which is above every name, that at the name of Jesus every knee should bow, in heaven and on earth and under the*

earth, and every tongue confess that Jesus Christ is Lord, to the glory of God the Father."

Chapter Five
STUDY GUIDE

*This Study Guide may be used for
personal meditation or group discussion.*

1. Have you ever had a "Less is More" experience in your life? Recall a time when this has been true for you and how the freedom of "less" influenced your life and spirit

2. Chapter Five opens with a very challenging question for all of us, "Are we ready and willing to live with 'less' in order that all might have 'more' according to God's kingdom provisions?" Take a moment to consider this tough question. Notice your automatic response.

3. What would choosing "LESS" look like in your life? What practical changes could you make today in order to free up more of your resources to give to others?

4. In what ways can you be a voice for those who have lost their voices in poverty, sickness or tragedy? How is God calling you to participate and be His source of answers to their cries for help?

IT'S BLOWING IN THE WIND

Chapter
Six

IT'S BLOWING IN THE WIND

In the summer of 2005 we watched in horror and disbelief as the winds of hurricane Katrina ripped across the Gulf Coast region of the United States. "Permanent" structures such as levees and buildings were tossed about and dismantled like toys by the awesome power of the storm. Such experiences remind us of our smallness in the universe, that we are not so powerful as we seem. One storm eroded decades of our progress; one day dismantled thousands of lives and livelihoods.

When strong winds come nothing remains unchanged. Invisible yet amazing in its power, wind can rearrange all that is in its path. A mighty wind comes in suddenly with a force all its own, creating its own conditions, reforming all landscape it touches. Gales easily blow giant, heavy ships across the sea. Wind-powered turbines provide electrical power to large metropolitan cities in many areas of the world. Wind is truly awesome in both its destructive and constructive power. It is no surprise then that our Creator God uses the tool and symbol of a mighty wind to represent His Holy Spirit.

We read of the coming of the Holy Spirit in Acts 2:1-3:

> *"When the day of Pentecost had come, they were all together in one place. And suddenly a sound came from heaven like the rush of a mighty wind, and it filled all the house where they were sitting. And there appeared to them tongues as of fire, distributed and resting on each one of them."*

Having witnessed the atoning death of Jesus on the cross, they were part of the greatest revolution against evil and the enemies of Jesus that this world has ever seen. These are the words of Jesus:

> *"But you shall receive power when the Holy Spirit has come upon you; and you shall be my witnesses in Jerusalem and in all Judea and Samaria and to the end of the earth."*
>
> ACTS 1:8

In the disasters of nature we see the destructive power of wind. But in God's wind of the Spirit there is wonder-working power. I have experienced the "constructive" power of wind that illustrates for me the movement of the Holy Spirit. Each year for 20 years I have participated in a Christian retreat in Bermuda. This tiny island, isolated in the Atlantic Ocean, is 22 miles long and one-and-a-half miles wide. With its 65 to 70 degree temperatures in January, flowers, shrubs and trees cause visitors to marvel at its breathtaking beauty. But for me, one of the most memorable features is the Bermuda wind. During my week there, I could depend on at least one day and night of the most powerful winds I have ever experienced. One night I was outside on my usual midnight walk. In the wind that night I was in danger of being blown down. I recall having a "shouting match" with the wind. I shouted praise to God, my Creator, for the wonder and majesty of His divine power. I also shouted prayers for His wind to blow through my being to cleanse me from all sin. I prayed:

"Spirit of the living God, Fall afresh on me:
Spirit of the living God, Fall afresh on me.
Melt me, mold me, fill me, use me,
Spirit of the living God, Fall afresh on me."

That night I was overwhelmed with the power of my Creator God. And more. The cleansing power of His new wind created within me praise beyond my ability to express. So I kept shouting praise to our Creator for many lives being lifted, blessed and healed in the Christian fellowship on this island paradise.

A postscript to this story is needed. Marta, my beloved life partner, was awakened by my midnight shouting outside our cabin. She thought she heard cries for help. She imagined me being blown into the rocks that lined the ocean shore. She came looking for her wounded husband, a victim of the Bermuda wind. How relieved she was to find that I was okay! It is interesting to note that she did not say, as many might have said, "Bill, why did you scare me like this? You shouldn't go walking late at night. I had a rough night because of you." Rather, with a hug, she showed gratitude that we were still together. Every day, especially at midnight, I thank God for the beauty of her body and spirit and for the gentle breeze of the spirit with which she refreshed my life.

Another postscript: Whether I was shouting at the wind or exclaiming "Hallelujah" in church, Marta did not object to having a "shouting Lutheran" in her life.

The wind of Bermuda reminded me in eloquent terms of the life-giving, life-transforming, life-sustaining wind of the Spirit of God. Some readers may ask, "If God uses His wind of the Spirit to do all these good things, why does He permit Katrina and Rita winds to destroy lives and property and cause indescribable suffering and pain to millions of persons?" Why *does* God allow such "destructive winds" into our lives?

We cannot get the answer to this question by human under-standing which is clouded by sin. We get the answer by divine reve-lation. Who better than our Creator can tell us who He is and of His perfect plan for us and for all creation? The sovereign and ultimate will of God is for perfection and paradise for every person He has created:

> *"Shower, O heavens, from above, and let the skies rain*
> *down righteousness; let the earth open, that salvation*
> *may sprout forth, and let it cause righteousness to spring up also;*
> *I the Lord have created it."*
> ISAIAH 45:8

However, we also need to consider God's permissive will. He has given us the gift of free will that makes us truly human. He did not create us as automatons, destined and forced to do His will. A forced goodness is contrived and superficial.

It is impossible to understand the meaning and purpose of suf-fering without the word "sin" in our vocabulary. We are persons born in sin that was inherited from our first parents. They dis-obeyed God, their Creator, and turned the paradise He intended for them and for all of us into a vale of tears, suffering and despair. But here is the good news; here comes the best out of the worst. In the midst of our suffering from the fall into sin comes the power of a suffering God and a Saviour who was crucified on a cross of torture and shame to rescue us for Paradise Regained.

And yet the question persists, "Why does your good and loving God permit these winds to blow terrible pain and suffering into our lives?" Some suffering comes from our free will choice of evil, as we choose to break the commandments of God which are written in the Bible, in us and in the very nature of the universe itself. We speak of breaking the law; we should speak of breaking ourselves against the law. This could be called "self-inflicted suffering".

Then there is what I would call "fallen world suffering". This kind of suffering baffles many. It creates questions such as, "Why do the innocent suffer?" There are destructive and death-dealing disasters on land, air and sea. There is the problem of widespread disease in an infected world. As a child I lived through the Spanish influenza epidemic of 1918. My friends and neighbors died. Can any good come out of such human disasters? Can anything good come out of the devastating winds in the Gulf area, out of a tsunami and terrifying death?

The answer is a resounding "Yes!" It's blowing in the wind, the Wind of the Holy Spirit, blowing new life and hope into every open heart.

We hear much about rebuilding the city of New Orleans, about rebuilding dikes, homes and infrastructures. Indeed, these are vital life and death plans, necessary for the survival of countless persons. But what shall it profit if all this rebuilding takes place and there is no rebuilding of persons, in spirit, mind and heart? Casinos, oil rigs, Bourbon Street and churches will be rebuilt. But how about new lives, new hearts, new attitudes, new divine plans? How about new efforts that will blow the lid off poverty areas and get rid of slum areas where victims of greed live? Will we build things "back to normal"? Is "normal" good enough?

Or will we let the winds of the Spirit of God blow divine love and purity and vision into us for healing of cities and persons? How can this come about? God has the answer in His Holy Word:

"If my people who are called by my name humble themselves,
and pray and seek my face, and turn from their wicked ways,
then I will hear from heaven,
and will forgive their sin and heal their land."
II CHRONICLES 7:14

The wind of the Spirit will bring a spirit of sorrow over our sins and bring healing to the land.

"When anyone is in Christ, there is a new world;
old things have passed away, the new has begun."
II CORINTHIANS 5:17 (MOFFAT)

Not only new persons, but a new world. It's blowing in the wind! In one of His resurrection appearances Jesus came to His fearful and confused disciples. Something new was blowing in the wind:

"Jesus said to them again, 'Peace be with you.
As the Father has sent me, even so I send you.'
And when he had said this, he breathed on them and said to them,
'Receive the Holy Spirit.'"
JOHN 20:21,22

In seeking to trust Jesus to bring the best out of the worst, it is impossible to get to God's best without the power of the Holy Spirit in our lives! Jesus himself acknowledged this when He said to His disciples:

"And I will ask the Father, and he will give you another
Counselor to be with you forever — the Spirit of truth.
The world cannot accept him, because it neither sees him
nor knows him. But you know him,
for he lives with you and will be in you."
JOHN 14:16,17 (NIV)

Therefore, as we seek to live as His witnesses, the power and presence of the Holy Spirit in our lives become a crucial focus.

In 1930, Dr. E. Stanley Jones wrote a book entitled, *The Christ of Every Road.* I read it in 1934 during my seminary years. This has been the best study on the Holy Spirit I have read. Here are some of the chapter titles: "The Lost Chord", "Pentecost and the Ordinary", "Pentecost and Sex", "Pentecost and Religious Imperialism", "Pentecost and Ritualism", "Pentecost and Material Possessions", "Pentecost and Modern Cults", "Pentecost and Environment", "Pentecost and the Christian Weapons", "Pentecost and Unity" and "Pentecost and the Morally Fit". I quote at some length from this book:

> "It (the church) is living between Easter and Pentecost. Easter stands for life wrought out, offered; Pentecost stands for life appropriated, lived to its full, unafraid and clearly and powerfully witnessing to an adequate way of human living. . .
>
> "We cannot imagine the Church with Pentecost eliminated. For there would have been no Church. Here the Church was born. True, there had been the period of gestation, for this holy thing lay within the womb of the purpose of God and was nourished by the life and teachings of Christ; the cross was the birth-pain; Easter heralded the coming birth, but Pentecost was the birthday. On that day was born the New Humanity. A new type of human being came into existence as different from ordinary humanity as ordinary humanity is different from the animal. . .
>
> "At Pentecost, this gospel came with them (the powers of Jesus), became identical with them — what they had heard and seen and what they were became one, hence they became irresistible apostles of a mighty passion."

Further, in his book entitled, *In Christ*, Dr. Jones writes:

> "The Holy Spirit was theirs potentially, but actually the Holy Spirit was not theirs until by surrender and faith they received the Holy Spirit at Pentecost when 'they were filled with the Holy Spirit.' Potentiality had become possession. Without that possession they would have lived on a promise, and it is possible to have a promise in your hands and be empty. . .It is possible to have possessions as a possibility, but the possessions are only possessions when you possess them. . .

"The dimness, the faintness, the dullness, the uncertainty of modern churchmen comes from believing in a salvation that is through Christ and not in Christ. They are living on the menu instead of the meat."

Living on the menu instead of the meat! Use your imagination for a moment. Suppose I am a waiter in a restaurant. You come in and sit down and I say, "Welcome to my restaurant. Here is the menu. Take your time and I'll be back in a few moments." Coming back a few moments later, I hear you say, "I'm ready to order." Then I say, "The food is all there on the menu before you." And you say, "Yes, I know, but I want the food that is described on the menu." "Sir, it's all there. You have it there!" Yes, you have the food potentially, as a possibility in your thoughts, but not as a possession. Indeed, many persons are trying to live on the menu instead of the meat. They know the words recorded in the Bible but not the Word Made Flesh. They are existing on potentialities and promises instead of on the actual possession of salvation in Christ and in the power of the Holy Spirit.

To avoid missing the power of the Holy Spirit in our lives, let us review His identity and His marks of leadership that make Him known in the world and in us, the followers of Jesus. Who is the Holy Spirit? How do we recognize Him at work? What can we expect from a life lived in the power of the Holy Spirit? God has gone out of His way to tell us.

The Holy Spirit — The Wind of Power

Today we witness an obsession for power — money power, political power, military power, media power, power of prestige and position. This is destructive wind power. King Solomon in Ecclesiastes 4:4 said:

"This also is vanity and a striving after wind."

Would you like to know about the redemptive power of suffering in your life? Read Romans 5:3-5. Are you interested in authentic love-power? Read again the Romans 5:3-5 passage. Would you like to be a messenger of the power of peace and a bringer of joy? Read Romans 14:17. Are you interested in the powerful gifts of music, joy and gratitude? Read Ephesians 5:18-21. Would you like to live an empowered life of service that can help build a better world? Read Acts 1:8.

Indeed, there is power, wonder-working power in the Wind of the Spirit!

THE HOLY SPIRIT — THE WIND OF TRUTH

There is only one way to know the Truth, only one way to be free from false doctrines that misinterpret the Word of God and from the teachings of false prophets, who lead people astray. It is the wind of the Spirit of Truth. We read about this in John 16:13:

"When the Spirit of Truth comes, he will guide you into all truth;
for he will not speak on his own authority,
but whatever he hears he will speak,
and he will declare to you the things that are to come."

It's blowing in the Wind of Truth!

THE HOLY SPIRIT — THE WIND OF AUTHORITY

In the midst of our frantic efforts to "run the world" by human technology and wisdom, we need to hear of the Lordship of Jesus Christ. He is Creator and Lord of the universe. He is Lord of the nations, Lord of history, Lord of the present and of the future. The question arises, "How can we truly believe that Jesus is Lord?" We have the answer in I Corinthians 12:3:

". . .and no one can say, '
Jesus is Lord' except by the Holy Spirit."

The Wind of True Authority in our lives and in our world!

THE HOLY SPIRIT — THE WIND OF COMFORT

In the midst of inevitable grief and sorrow and suffering in this fallen world, friends seek to comfort us and we are grateful. Comfort is also found in the shedding of tears. Friends pray for us and that surely helps, but there is only One who can bring true and lasting relief from distress and ills of the spirit. In Romans 8:26-27, we read:

> *"Likewise the Spirit helps us in our weakness; for we do not know how to pray as we ought, but the Spirit himself intercedes for us with sighs too deep for words. And he who searches the hearts of men knows what is the mind of the Spirit, because the Spirit intercedes for the saints according to the will of God."*

I recall a conversation with an elderly woman in a care center. She had many impairments in her body. I reminded her that Jesus was praying for her and the Holy Spirit was praying for her. I shall never forget her response: "Then how can I lose!"

The Wind of Comfort — too deep for words!

THE HOLY SPIRIT — THE WIND OF CONVICTION

Sometimes we are tempted to think that our human words and convictions can help people to know the Truth and realities of life. Our words fail and fade, especially in the light of the gift of the Holy Spirit of whom it is written in John 16:7-11:

> *"Nevertheless I tell you the truth: it is to your advantage that I go away, for if I do not go away, the Counselor will not come to you; but if I go, I will send him to you. And when he comes, he will convince the world concerning sin and righteousness and judgment: concerning sin, because they do not believe in me; concerning righteousness, because I go to the Father, and you will see me no more; concerning judgment, because the ruler of this world is judged."*

Many witnesses for Christ have been hindered in their sharing of the gospel message by feelings of inadequacy or an inability to articulate the message convincingly. Jesus comes to us saying that the Holy Spirit, not our words, holds the power to convince. Therefore, we can share our faith with joy and remain confident witnesses, leaving the results to God alone.

The Wind of Conviction — God's redeeming wind alive in the world today!

THE HOLY SPIRIT — THE WIND OF THE SPIRIT IS GOD'S BEST GIFT

Many are willing to settle for what they call good gifts as they reject the best gift, the highest honor, to be called worthy to receive the gift of a fruitful and fulfilling life, bringing hope and joy to many others. The Holy Spirit guides us with love, joy, peace, patience, kindness, goodness, faithfulness, gentleness and self-control in our lives, causing us to be people bearing gifts of God's love to the world.

God's Best Gift! It's blowing in the wind!

Through receiving the gift of God's Holy Spirit we can indeed trust and know that God will bring the best out of the worst in our lives! May we welcome His Spirit in us as we trust Him and receive His presence in our lives. The late Pastor Ross Foley, who served for many years as Pastor of Faith Covenant Church in Burnsville, Minnesota, voices this desire for all of us in his exciting sermon about Pentecost:

> "So I say, welcome to Pentecost! It's time to open up the mind-blowing, heart-warming, life-changing power of God. The power of God can invade the body, inflate the mind, swell the soul, lift the spirit, and make us more than we ever imagined. The Holy Spirit will make you young when you're old. He'll make you live when you die. The power and presence of the Spirit will disturb, delight, and deliver us from sin.
>
> "When God sends forth the Spirit, chaos is changed into creation. The Red Sea opens up into a highway to freedom. A young woman says, 'Yes.' Jesus is born and life is never the same. When God sends forth the Spirit, amazing things happen. Barriers are broken. Communities are formed. Opposites are reconciled. Unity is established. Disease is cured. Addiction is

broken. Cities are renewed. Races are reconciled. Hope is established. People are blessed. And church happens.

"Today the Spirit of God is present as He is every time we come to worship. So be ready. Get ready. God is up to something. Discouraged folks, cheer up. Dishonest folks, 'fess up'. Sour folks, sweeten up. Closed folks, open up. Gossipers, shut up. Conflicted folks, make up. Sleeping folks, wake up. Lukewarm folks, fire up. Dry bones, shake up. Pew potatoes, stand up. But most of all, when the Holy Spirit is present, Christ the Savior of the world is lifted up."

This is the Spirit that Christ gives to our hurting world, to our lost and wounded souls. Can we trust this Jesus, who gives us His Spirit? Yes, we can.

We can trust Him and we can come to Him just as we are. We do not need to clean up, recover or rebuild before we come to Jesus. He comes to us in our worst moments, when we are ashamed, lost and dying inside and out. According to His Word, He comes "to seek and to save the lost". It is His power, His Holy Spirit, who makes us right and righteous before God. The power of the Holy Spirit is the power to live.

Three examples follow: one from the life of Billy Graham, one from the life of a woman set free from addiction and one from the life of a man in whom the Holy Spirit kept God alive.

The story is told of Billy Graham visiting a local congregation to preach. Before the service, one of the deacons met him and said, "Dr. Graham, I should inform you that we have had turmoil and trouble here recently. One of our members came to church intoxicated and we had to drop him as a member."

Billy Graham replied, "That's interesting. May I ask what you do when one of your members fails to be filled with the Spirit?" The startled deacon asked, "What do you mean?" Billy replied, "The Bible says in Ephesians 5:18, 'And do not get drunk with wine, for that is debauchery; but be filled with the Holy Spirit.' Now when one of your members who is drunk with wine comes to church, you expel him. But do you keep on welcoming members who refuse

Jesus' offer of His indwelling Presence in the Person of the Holy Spirit?" Evidently the leaders of that church had not moved on to Pentecost. With the Holy Spirit guiding and empowering them, they could have surrounded their erring brother as fellow sinners and helped him find freedom from his addiction.

Serving in an inner city church in Minneapolis from 1965 to 1980, I witnessed firsthand the power of the Holy Spirit to rescue such persons struggling with addictions. One of the very important organizations in this parish was called the "A-Plus Group", a Christ-centered, Holy Spirit-empowered program to help persons seeking freedom from their addictive bondage. The leader of this group herself had led a sordid life until she came to complete healing and liberation through a personal encounter with Jesus Christ as her Lord and Saviour. She introduced the group members to Jesus who died to make people free. She was experiencing the power of the Holy Spirit in her life.

In the last example, an anti-social newcomer moved into a rural community. He put up a fence around his property and "No Trespassing" signs to warn all intruders. To insure his privacy he put a fierce dog behind that fence. One day his next-door neighbor's little girl crawled under the fence to pet the dog, and that fierce beast grasped her by the throat and killed her.

The community was enraged. They ostracized the unfriendly neighbor. No one spoke to him. Clerks refused to wait on him. In the spring no one would sell him grain for his fields. He was destitute. One day he looked out to see another man sowing seed in his field. He rushed to that man only to discover it was the father of the little girl. "Why are you doing this, you of all people?" "I am doing it," said the father, "to keep God alive in me."

Receiving the ministry and power of the Holy Spirit is vital then, not only for you and me but also for others in order to bear fruit. This is a costly faith. It will cost you your life. The price is surrender of all that you are and all that you have to Jesus, who gave His life for you. Then you can say with Saint Paul in Philippians 4:13:

"I can do everything God asks me to with the help of Christ who
gives me the strength and power." (TLB)

Ready for anything! It's blowing in the wind! In our journey of faith, we move from incarnation (God with us—Christmas) to redemption (God for us — Easter) to sanctification (God in us — Pentecost). And this is what the Bible says in Colossians 1:27b:

"Christ in you, the hope of glory!"

Chapter Six
STUDY GUIDE

*This Study Guide may be used for
personal meditation or group discussion.*

1. At times it can be easier to believe in human perspectives rather than in divine inspiration. Do you believe in the Holy Spirit and God's power to bring new life and hope to all who trust Jesus? Explain.

2. What are some areas in your own life into which you would like to invite the Holy Spirit's wind to blow anew?

3. Name some of the "winds of change" that you are aware of in the world today. How might these winds be in agreement with or contrary to the wind of the Holy Spirit at work in the world?

4. How might choosing to listen to and observe the Holy Spirit at work be part of God's best gift for you and for the world? What differences might come about as a result of allowing the Holy Spirit to come in, according to the Bible? See:

   Acts 2:1-3
   John 20:21-22
   John 14:16-17
   John 16:13-14
   I Corinthians 2:3
   Romans 8:26-27
   Psalm 51:10-13

EPILOGUE

According to the dictionary the word epilogue means "something more — in addition". Someone may ask, "Haven't you said enough?" My reply is, "Well, I have tried to answer the questions that are presented in the Preface of this book, to give answers from the scriptures and from life. At the age of 95, this book could well be the last book that I write. It is my conviction that something more needs to be said before the book is finished. (As much as any book can ever be finished.)

I know that if I permit Jesus to open my mind to understand the Scriptures, and if I am faithful to His Word, this "something more to be added" will be a blessing to readers. Hopefully, many will enter into this "heart-to-heart" reflection time and read on.

Two of the questions for which we have sought answers in the book are: "Where were God and His Son Jesus in the destructive disasters of nature?" and "Why does God permit them to happen, bringing such indescribable suffering to so many persons?" We have not looked to philosophers, theologians and human judgments for opinions and perspectives. Hopefully, additional and more reassuring answers will come through the questions we now present to our readers.

The first question comes from the title of the book, *Trust Jesus to Bring the Best Out of the Worst,* and especially from the first two words, ***Trust Jesus.***

When you say,
" I believe in Jesus, my Saviour and Lord,"
do you trust Him to take perfect care of your life?

Believing and trusting are inseparable facets of our Christian faith, and yet, though intricately connected, they are not entirely the same thing.

I recall the story of a high-wire performer who walked on a wire stretched between mountain peaks over a rocky mountain gorge. A huge audience far below watched in amazement and in fright over the possibilities of his falling. His next feat was to walk across, not with his balancing rod, but pushing a wheelbarrow. He then came down to the ground and said to his admirers, "Do you think that I can push a wheelbarrow across the gorge with a person in it?" The response was unanimous, "You can't do it! You won't try it!" Unanimous except for one man who came forward and said, "I believe you can do it. I know you can do it! You can do anything up there on that high wire!" The performer said, "Thank you, sir, for having confidence in me. We will go up the mountain together and you will get into the wheelbarrow."

Indeed, it is easy to say, "I believe." Superficial, shallow faith often makes this affirmation. Somehow, it is more reassuring for me to say in the title of this book, *Trust Jesus to Bring the Best Out of the Worst* than *Believe that Jesus Can Bring the Best Out of the Worst*. Inevitably the question presses upon us, "Is not believing in Jesus as our Lord and Saviour sufficient?"

Saint Paul writes in Romans 5:1:

"Therefore, since we are justified by faith, we have peace with God through our Lord, Jesus Christ."

We read in John 3:16:

*". . .that whoever **believes** in him shall not perish but have eternal life."*

In John 11:40 we recall these words of Jesus to Martha at the grave of her brother Lazarus:

*"Did I not tell you that if you would **believe** you would see the glory of God."*

And if ever you wanted an impressive list of the great leaders of the people of God and how they survived by faith, read Hebrews, chapter 11. In Hebrews 11:6 we read:

*"And without faith it is impossible to please him. For whoever would draw near to God must **believe** that he exists and that he rewards those who seek him."*

In Acts 16:31, Saint Paul answers the question of the Philippian jailer, "What must I do to be saved?" with these words:

*"**Believe** in the Lord Jesus,
and you will be saved, you and your household."*

In I John 5:13 we learn that those who believe in the name of Jesus will know that they have eternal life.

Justification by faith is a cardinal doctrine in my Church. We believe in faith alone, grace alone, the Word alone. In the light of the eternal truths of scripture, how can I say that we need something more than faith to be saved? That is not what I am saying. What I am trying to say is that we need to know more about faith and what it means.

Faith or belief in something or someone initially reflects an intellectual, emotional and/or spiritual assent. We can have faith in the chair that we sit on; we can believe that it will hold us up, but until we sit on it, until we rest our full weight on it, we have not exercised faith. **Trust, then, is the experience of coming to rest our whole selves on the faith that we acclaim.** It is into such trusting faith as this that Jesus invites us.

Growing from faith into trust may not be an easy step to take. Come with me to an imaginary scene at the John F. Kennedy Air Terminal in New York City. My wife, Marta, and I are ready to board a 747 plane bound for Europe. I am skeptical about flying. I ask, "How many will be on this plane?" She replies, "370 persons." "Will they take all of our baggage?" I ask. "Of course," she replies. Then I said, "I am not going." She said, "Why not?" My answer, "Because I believe in the law of gravity. This huge hulk of steel cannot defy the law of gravity and go up." Now Marta is very intelligent. She is also very patient with me. She said, "I too believe in the law of gravity. But there is a higher law. We call it the law of aerodynamics." She explained this law to me. So, trusting Marta and her guidance, I get on board. And we go up. Now (here we must let our imagination wander widely), suppose out over the Atlantic Ocean, I say, "Honey, it's very hot and stuffy in here. I think I'll go out for some air." Suppose that somehow I could get out of the plane. At that moment

I am no longer under the higher law of aerodynamics. I come under the control of the lower law of gravity. I do not stay up. I go down into the ocean.

Preposterous you say. Perhaps. The point is that faith is essential to get us to our destination. Faith in what? In a higher law? No, in a higher Person. In the Creator who has given us His laws of the universe.

In every earthbound realm we surely travel by faith. In fact, we would not take a single step on the journey without faith. Here are some examples: As you eat your breakfast cereal, do you wonder if dog food has been mixed in? You eat all of your food by faith, yes, by faith in persons you have never seen. When you get on a plane, do you check the pilots for their credentials? Do you check the flight deck to see if they are all there? Rather I think that you sit down and place your life in the hands of strangers. Lavish faith indeed! I have been wheeled into operating rooms seven different times in my life. I probably have met the surgeon. The nurses and attendants are all strangers. By faith I will let the doctor make cuts into this one precious body I have. That is putting my very life on the line of faith!

God's Word has much to say regarding the connection between faith and trust.

Many believe in weapons of war. In Psalm 20:7 (GNT) we read:

*"Some **trust** in their war chariots and others in their horses, but we **trust** in the power of the Lord our God."*

And in Psalm 37:5 (GNT):

*"Give yourself to the Lord; **trust** in him, and he will help you."*

We read about trust in Isaiah 26:4(GNT):

*"**Trust** in the Lord forever; he will always protect us."*

A further word from Isaiah 12:2(GNT):

*"God is my Savior; I will **trust** him and not be afraid. The Lord gives me power and strength; he is my Savior."*

In The Living Bible paraphrase of Psalm 50:15 we find these words:

*"I want you to **trust** me in your times of trouble,
so I can rescue you, and you can give me glory."*

Dear reader, you say that you believe. That is good. But is your faith strong enough for you to entrust your life and future to Him in whom you believe? Can you say with Saint Paul in II Timothy 1:12:

*"I know whom I have believed, and I am sure that he is able
to guard until that Day what has been entrusted to me."*

As I am obsessed with the first two words of the title of this book, *Trust Jesus*, I hope and pray that it is a magnificent obsession for the glory of my Lord.

A second question often asked concerns doubt.

Is it okay to doubt Jesus and His promises?

We know that our faith, and surely our trust, can often waver. At such times, it is more important than ever to know the heart of God. Jesus and His Word and His dealing with doubt in the lives of his followers reveals much about God's heart. Recognizing their human sinful condition, Jesus never judged honest doubters as being lost, but rather, in His Amazing Grace, always brought something good out of the inevitable struggles of believing.

However, there were certain doubters for whom Jesus had strong words of caution. He called the doubting Scribes and Pharisees hypocrites. They rejected Jesus as the Son of God and planted doubts about His life and work. They were using their doubts as "smoke screens" behind which they could hide their self-righteousness and their rejection of truth.

And if we believe in the reality of evil in our fallen world and in the prince of darkness, Satan, who poisons the mind, cripples the feelings and perverts the will, then it will be clear that he plants destructive doubts in the hearts of believers. Indeed, he planted doubts in the hearts of Adam and Eve with this question:

"Did God say, 'You shall not eat of any tree of the garden?'"
GENESIS 3:1

As they heeded the voice of the tempter, great indeed was their fall and the fall of all creation into suffering, sorrow, pain, doubt and fear.

How did Jesus deal with doubt? Some theologians and scholars believe that Jesus taught that we should never doubt the reality of God's goodness and grace and power in the midst of terrible suffering and evil. John Piper, in his book, *Taste and See*, comments on Jesus' prediction of the "terrors" that will be coming upon the world as described in Luke, chapter 21. He writes, "In spite of all this evil and suffering, Jesus did not even remotely suggest that we should have a flicker of doubt toward the goodness and sovereignty of God."

He goes on to quote the words of Jesus in Luke 21:31: "'*When you see these things taking place, you know that the kingdom of God is near.*' This is not the suggestion of doubt but the certainty of hope. This is not a time for weakening faith, but unwavering hope." Indeed, Jesus does not condone doubt or indicate that it is a good gift, even though He can use it for good. However, let us now see what Jesus does with inevitable doubts, anger and fears that beset all of human nature.

At His resurrection, Jesus appeared to His disciples who, on seeing His crucifixion scars, believed and rejoiced. One disciple, Thomas, was absent that day. When the disciples told him they had seen the Lord, he said in John 20:25, "*Unless I see in his hands the print of the nails, and place my finger in the mark of the nails, and place my hand in his side, I will not believe.*" Eight days later Jesus said to Thomas in John 20:27, "*Put your finger here, and see my hands; and put out your hand, and place it in my side; do not be faithless, but believing.*" Thomas answered Him, "*My Lord and my God!*" (vs. 28)

In Matthew 14, we read of Jesus appearing to His disciples in their boat as He walked on the water toward them. Accepting Jesus' invitation, the impetuous Peter climbed out of the boat and started walking on the water towards Jesus. Suddenly, in the midst of the wind and waves, he began to sink and cried out: "*Lord, save me.*"

Jesus immediately reached out his hand and caught him, saying to him, *"O man of little faith, why did you doubt?"* The story ends with the disciples worshipping Jesus with these words, *"Truly you are the Son of God."*(vs. 30,31,33). Indeed, Jesus recognized doubt in the lives of His people and yet redeemed them for His glory.

And what an Almighty, Creator God we have as He listens patiently to His servant Job, in whose life He had permitted Satan to bring unspeakable family tragedies and terrifying physical suffering. As Job cries out in despair, he questions and doubts God. Job says in verse 11 of chapter 7, *"Therefore I will not restrain my mouth; I will speak in the anguish of my spirit; I will complain in the bitterness of my soul."* He goes on to say in verses 20 and 21, *"If I sin, what do I do to thee, thou watcher of men? Why hast thou made me thy mark? Why have I become a burden to thee? Why doest thou not pardon my transgression and take away my iniquity? For now I shall lie in the earth; thou wilt seek me, but I shall not be."* Later we hear Job's shout of faith and victory in chapter 19:25, *"I know that my redeemer lives."*

Have I ever doubted Jesus and His promises? What happened to these doubts?

In the midst of deep differences of opinion among scholars and theologians concerning the place of doubt in the lives of believers, I will now say that I have never doubted God or Jesus or the Holy Spirit in my journey of faith. I should add that this journey has been filled with tough spiritual battles and struggles, but they never ended in doubting God and Jesus and Divine love. Amidst all that is uncertain in this world, there is one thing that we can know for sure, one thing that we need never doubt, and that is the character of God. Regardless of circumstances, perceptions, emotions, faith or faithlessness, the true and loving character of God remains unchanged and unchanging, our steady center in a world of constant chaos and change.

My own journey throughout the years has revealed and solidified this truth for me. Those who have a copy of my book, *Show Me the*

Way to Go Home — Journey to the Promised Land, hopefully have read Chapter 28, "What I Learned About Running". As I have written there and now write in this "Epilogue", my spiritual struggle has been in the realm of **self-doubt**. There may be some confusion between doubt and self-doubt. With self-doubt, I doubt my capacity to believe the promises of God. Does this mean that I doubt God or tone down my song of praise? No indeed! Here is my song of praise that takes me beyond self-doubt to the blessed assurance of Jesus' Word. He is able to move us from doubt and perplexity to praise.

"Now to him who by the power at work within us is able to
do far more abundantly than all we ask or think, to him be glory
in the church and in Christ Jesus to all generations,
for ever and ever. Amen."
EPHESIANS 3:20, 21

In the midst of self-doubt, I have never doubted the basic truths as revealed in the Bible. I have never doubted the sovereignty of God. I have never doubted the teaching of Jesus on His incarnation, His becoming the Word made Flesh. I have never doubted His act of redemption on a cross of suffering and pain. I have never doubted the coming of the Holy Spirit to live within me, God in me, my hope of glory.

Please come with me on a journey to the place of self-doubt.

This struggle began early in my life. One summer I was raking hay in a Michigan field. As I recall, I was about 12 or 13 years old. It was a one horse operation. On that hot and humid day, all alone in that field, I was overwhelmed with a sense of estrangement and lostness. I experienced the blackness of despair. I wondered if salvation for me was possible. In the days following, I bargained with God. If He would forgive and save me, I would follow in the steps of my father and become a minister.

Later, in the small town of Tustin, Michigan, I was sitting in a Presbyterian Church listening to George B. Bernard who was famous for writing the words and music of the hymn, "The Old Rugged Cross". He played and sang this song that night. He preached with

Holy Spirit power the love of Jesus for sinners. He painted a terrifying picture of the consequences of unforgiven and unconfessed sin. But this only magnified his picture of the price Jesus paid on the cross of terrifying torture and shame to save all penitent sinners. At the time of the altar call, a number of my high school friends went forward, together with many adults. The Holy Spirit was nudging me to go forward. To this day I knew that I should have made this move and surrendered my life publicly to the Lord, but I sat there enveloped in self-doubt. "I am the preacher's son, do I need saving?" (My father was a Lutheran pastor in that town, and I am sure he was hoping that I would go forward.) I doubted if I could live up to such a decision. And I kept running through the rest of my high school and college days, running from the Lord.

I came home from college just six hours before my father died. I sat by his death bed. Though in a coma, I knew his spirit was still praying for me. There I surrendered my life to Jesus, a great big sinner saved by Amazing Grace, saved for a lifetime of service for Him and for others.

Years later, I recall one of our Christian Ashram tours to India. As leader of our tour group, I spent freely of my time and energy and at the end of the tour I was "spent". I came down from the Ashram Mother House in the Himalayan Mountains on a long, hot and humid ride of several hundred miles to Lucknow, India. I arrived there dehydrated, exhausted and full of self-doubt. I recall going into the beautiful sanctuary of the United Methodist Church in Lucknow. There I saw a sign that read, "Here Stanley Jones, servant of God, knelt, a sick man, ready to return to America as a failed missionary. Here he prayed and surrendered his life anew to Jesus. Here he arose, completely well and whole, and for the next sixty years lifted up Jesus to millions of people on every continent." And there at the altar of that church I knelt and cried out, "Lord have mercy upon me." There I surrendered my problems, struggles and self-doubts to Him. I arose well and whole, reinvigorated and filled with divine power, not only for the rest of that journey but for every succeeding problem with self-doubt.

*"He himself bore our sins in his body on the tree,
that we might die to sin and live to righteousness.
By his wounds you have been healed."*
I PETER 2:24

God uses Scripture as an amazing tool against our self-doubt. Once I was on a plane flying from New York to Scotland to begin a three-month study tour which would take me to Scotland, Scandinavia, Germany and Switzerland. The year was 1962. My national church, which I had been serving for 11 years as Director of Evangelism, was merging with several other Lutheran bodies. This merged church became known as Lutheran Church in America. The headquarters was moving from Minneapolis to New York. Many hours that night on the plane I struggled with self-doubt. Am I ready and willing to go to New York to work in the new headquarters there? Am I ready to go back into the parish as a parish pastor? The same promise came to me from Psalm 32:8. It brought peace and blessed assurance.

*"I will instruct you and teach you the way you should go;
I will counsel you with my eye upon you."*

Then I read Psalm 91:15,16:

*"When he calls to me, I will answer him;
I will be with him in trouble, I will rescue him and honor him.
With long life I will satisfy him, and show him my salvation."*

Oh yes, self-doubt still besets me. I could not survive unless I could go daily to the throne of grace and there in confession and absolution receive forgiveness and pardon. And also acquittal for every sin that I daily commit.

We who wrestle with self-doubt must often return to what is the very heart and center of this book — the cross of Jesus and His suffering and death, there to atone for our sins. In one way or another we have repeated in this book the thought, "Out of the worst tragedy that ever happened in the universe, when we nailed the Son of God on the cross, came the best, redemption and God's unconditional love. Jesus' Good Shepherd presence sustains us every step of the way. Indeed, the best out of the worst!

Each morning in my devotions I sing several songs in connection with praising our Lord for a long list of blessings. One of the blessings that I never miss is "The Blessing of The Way". Jesus said in John 14:6:

"I am the way, the truth and the life;
no one comes to the Father, but by me."

Then I sing a verse of a song written by Dr. Samuel Miller:

"Jesus only on the mountain,
Jesus only on the sea,
Jesus only in the valley,
There in dark Gethsemane.
Jesus only up to Calvary,
Jesus only on the cross,
Jesus only in all suffering,
All things else are empty dross."

I think of Jesus in Gethsemane and on the cross, in terrifying agony of spirit as God was placing our sin and guilt and the evil of all the world in his body, separating Him from His Heavenly Father. Then I hear Him cry, *"Father, if it be possible, let this cup pass from me, not as I will but as thou will,"* and I thank the Lord for the Friend who died for me.

"Greater love has no man than this,
that a man lay down his life for his friends.
You are my friends if you do what I command you."
JOHN 15:13,14

As I keep looking at the cross, a big sinner like me with my sins of self-doubt and self-vindication, I cannot help but trust Him. No, I do not doubt Jesus. I doubt myself and may doubt some who claim to be His followers, but never Jesus.

I am finishing this chapter on the night of Ash Wednesday. This night my Lord and Saviour met me in the Holy Place of His presence and He said, "This is my body given for you. This is my blood shed for you." I came to Him as a sinner singing the song in my spirit, "Just As I Am Without One Plea". As I returned to my place of worship in the sanctuary, I rejoiced in the knowledge of my Lord and Saviour. Not only is He with me but He lives within me. As I take the bread and wine in my physical body, I receive Jesus' Holy Presence in my spirit. These words came to me, Philippians 4:13: (J.B. PHILLIPS)

> *"I am ready for anything in the strength*
> *of the one who lives within me."*

Oh yes! In the impressive service with the imposition of the ashes, I was marked with the cross and the words, *"From dust thou art and to dust thou shall return."* Is this an unhappy thought — I return to dust? No indeed! It magnifies our Lord's Amazing Grace, that through our dust and ashes, our self-doubt, our lostness, He can bring forth our resurrected bodies to live in the presence of Jesus in our Eternal Home forever and ever.

And to think that my Lord marked me with this same cross of His love after I was born into this world! He nurtured me in the faith in which I came to accept His acceptance of me, a sinner. I thank my Lord for the covenant He made with me in my baptism.

In the Preface and throughout the course of this book we have asked several questions:

Where were God and Jesus when the many disasters took place?
If not Jesus, who do you think can bring the best out of the worst?
Do you settle for the good that we can do rather than for the best that Jesus can do?
If Jesus is my friend, why does He not take me out of my suffering?

For answers, we have turned together to the highest authority, God's Word. We read in Luke 24:25:

"Then he (Jesus) opened their minds to understand the scriptures."

The key words in this book are **trust Jesus**. To trust Jesus means to obey Him and to become involved in servanthood fulfilled for His glory. Jesus gives an impressive example:

"Then he poured water into a basin, and began to wash the disciples' feet, and to wipe them with the towel with which he was girded."
JOHN 13:5

After meeting Peter's objections to Jesus washing his feet, Jesus said:

"If I then, your Lord and Teacher, have washed your feet,
you also ought to wash one another's feet.
For I have given you an example,
that you also should do as I have done to you."
JOHN 13:14,15

To trust Jesus means doing something for Him. It means finding persons in need and serving them with Jesus' love and in His name. We need the reminder in I Chronicles 28:20:

"Then David said to Solomon his son, 'Be strong and
of good courage, and do it. Fear not, be not dismayed;
for the Lord God, even my God, is with you. He will not
fail you or forsake you, until all the work for the service
of the house of the Lord is finished.'"

It is appropriate for me to close this chapter and book with my eyes on the cross and on the risen Saviour. Each day in my devotions and spirit, I hear the sound of hammer blows nailing Jesus to a cross of torture where He died in my place and for my sins. I hear His cry, *"It is finished!"* and thank Him for His finishing work in the world, in the Church, in the land and in my 95 years of life.

"For God took the sinless Christ and poured into him our sins.
Then, in exchange, he poured God's goodness into us!"
II CORINTHIANS 5:21 (TLB)

"Now glory be to God who by his mighty power at
work within us is able to do far more than we would

ever dare to ask or even dream of — infinitely beyond our highest prayers, desires, thoughts, or hopes. May he be given glory forever and ever through endless ages because of his master plan of salvation for the church through Jesus Christ." EPHESIANS 3:20, 21(TLB)

Indeed, Jesus brings the best out of the worst!!

A Final Challenge to Trust Jesus

As we seek to bring terrorists and violators of human rights to justice, will we bring ourselves to repentance, depending upon the Holy Spirit to make this possible?

"If my people who are called by my name humble themselves,
and pray and seek my face, and turn from their wicked ways,
then I will hear from heaven,
and will forgive their sin and heal their land.
II Chronicles 7:14

When will we recognize that the root cause of all the "worsts" in human history is the sin of unbelief, the sin of rejecting the commandments and the teachings of Jesus? When will we be aware that sin is the cause of the Aids epidemic, global warming and all broken human relationships?

Sin, an unpopular and neglected word, defines who we are. Sin means separation from God, estrangement, a broken relationship. Sin is bondage to the old nature. Sin is a condition of the human heart, infected and polluted. Out of our evil nature come specific acts of sin.

"For out of the heart come evil thoughts, murder,
adultery, fornication, theft, false witness, slander."
Matthew 15:19

If sin is our major problem, what can we do about it? We can **trust Jesus** as our Saviour from sin and accept His power to live for Him and for others.

"For our sake he made him to be sin who knew no sin,
so that in him we might become the righteousness of God."
II Corinthians 5:21

When will human manifestos for freedom and justice fade in the light of Jesus' Divine Manifesto?

"The Spirit of the Lord is upon me, because he has

anointed me to preach good news to the poor. He has sent me to proclaim release to the captives and recovering of sight to the blind, to set at liberty those who are oppressed, to proclaim the acceptable year of the Lord."
LUKE 4:18,19

Will we **trust Jesus** and heed His words in the midst of our fear of things that are and things to come?

"And there will be signs in sun and moon and stars, and upon the earth distress of nations in perplexity at the roaring of the sea and the waves, men fainting with fear and with foreboding of what is coming on the world; for the powers of the heavens will be shaken. And then they will see the Son of man coming in a cloud with power and great glory. Now when these things begin to take place, look and raise your heads, because your redemption is drawing near."
LUKE 21:25-28

In the midst of wars and other tragedies and in the midst of human suffering and pain, will we see redemption drawing near from our Lord?

Will we turn our eyes to the cross where Jesus brought the best out of the worst?

Will you, dear reader, claim by faith the divine promise in Romans 8:32:

"He who did not spare his own son but gave him up for us all, will he not also give us all things with Him?"

THANK YOU

To the members of my family. They have been indispensable partners and supporters and encouragers in the almost endless writing and rewriting process. I thank our Lord for each one, Anne and J. Paul Carlson; Bill, Karen, Will and Ben Berg; Jon, Mari and Emery Carlson; Jeff Carlson, Monica Mesa and Maya Carlson; Katie and Matt Schoeppner; Steven Conrad; Karen and David Balmer; Paul Conrad and Mary Brainard.

To countless friends who have been praying for this ministry. Their oft-repeated words, "We're looking forward to reading your book," have been a blessed affirmation for me.

To Marta Berg, my life partner for 55 years. The poems from her books of narrative verse that have appeared in all of my books, have surely been highlights of inspiration and challenge. More than a brilliant writer, the inspiration of her presence in spirit with me has helped me greatly in my continuing ministry. In 1996 she became one of the Saints in Glory.

To the members of the editing committee: Katherine Krause, Anne Carlson, Carol Smith, Jon Carlson, Katie Schoeppner, Heather Halen, Don and Karin Goodell. These friends have spent hours and days in reading, rereading and correcting the manuscript. For sheer skill and accuracy, I believe that these friends could more than hold their own with any editorial committee in the employment of well-known publishers.

To Katherine Krause, one of the editors of the book, who is an outstanding writer and poet. Katherine has given us permission to quote from her writings

To Rae Ann Foley, who gave us permission to quote from one of her deceased husband, Ross Foley's sermons. Ross was a great preacher who proclaimed heavenly truths in down-to-earth terms. His thoughts in this book are powerful.

To Perry Duff Smith, Jr. of Koechel Peterson & Associates and Bronze Bow Publishing, for his work on the final cover design and interior layout. His professional guidance in the long journey toward publication has given me confidence and assurance.

To David Koechel of Koechel, Peterson & Associates and Bronze Bow Publishing, for his work on the cover illustration and design. He also provided indispensable help and guidance in the printing and publication of this book. To visit their headquarters and to witness the amazing work they do, not only for Christian publishers but for many others, is indeed a memorable event.

To Carol Smith for her almost endless typing and retyping of corrected manuscripts and for her outstanding editing skills. She has shown patience and poise under the pressure of deadlines and has spent hours as a research specialist in securing copyright privileges. She has been a partner in my writing ministry for whom I thank our Lord, no less than a gift from our Lord.

To the authors and publishers of quotations in this book for permission to include their copyrighted messages. These are acknowledged in another section.

Above all, I give praise to my Lord and Saviour for permitting me to write this book at the age of 95 (and 96).

Indeed, to God be the glory!

ACKNOWLEDGMENTS

Taken from *Ruthless Trust, The Ragamuffin's Path to God* by Brennan Manning. Copyright © 2000 by Brennan Manning. Used by permission of Harper/San Francisco, a Division of Harper Collins Publishers (page xv).

Taken from *Seen & Unseen* by Marta Berg. Copyright © 1991 by Marta Berg. Winston-Derek Publishers, Inc. (page xvii).

Taken from a sermon entitled "The Supremacy of Christ in an Age of Terror" by John Piper. Used by permission (pages 3, 4).

Taken from *Is the Kingdom of God Realism* by E. Stanley Jones. Copyright © MCMXL by Whitmore and Stone, Publishers. Used by permission of Eunice Mathews, daughter of the late E. Stanley Jones (pages 4, 5).

Taken from *The Christ of the Indian Road* by E. Stanley Jones. Copyright © 1925 by E. Stanley Jones. Used by permission of Eunice Mathews, daughter of the late E. Stanley Jones (pages 5, 6).

Taken from *My Utmost for His Highest* by Oswald Chambers. Copyright © 1935 by Dodd Mead & Co., renewed 1963 by the Oswald Chambers Publications Assn. Ltd., and is used by permission of Discovery House Publishers, Box 3566, Grand Rapids, MI 49501. All rights reserved (page 22).

Taken from *The Word Became Flesh* by E. Stanley Jones. Copyright © 1963 by Abingdon Press. Used by permission of Abingdon Press (page 24).

Taken from "Spirit of the Living God." Copyright © by Daniel Iverson. Arrangement copyright © 1934 by Herbert G. Tovey (page 61).

Taken from *The Christ of Every Road* by E. Stanley Jones. Copyright © 1930 by E. Stanley Jones. Used by permission of Eunice Mathews, daughter of the late E. Stanley Jones (page 65).

Taken from *In Christ* by E. Stanley Jones. Copyright © by Abingdon Press. Used by permission of Abingdon Press (pages 65, 66).

Taken from a sermon given on a Pentecost Sunday by the late Pastor Ross Foley. Used by permission (pages 69, 70).

Taken from *Taste and See* by John Piper. Copyright © 1999, 2005 by Desiring God Foundation. Published by Multnomah Publishers, Inc. (page 80).

"Jesus Only" taken from *Youth's Favorite Songs*. Copyright © Samuel M. Miller (Page 85).

In Public Domain

Taken from "My Hope is Built on Nothing Less" from the Lutheran Book of Worship (Page 16).

Taken from "There is a Fountain Filled With Blood" from the Lutheran Book of Worship (Page 29).

Taken from "Jesus Keep Me Near the Cross" from the Lutheran Book of Worship (Page 29).

Taken from "When Peace Like a River" from the Lutheran Book of Worship (Page 42).

Taken from "More Love to Thee" from the Lutheran Book of Worship (Page 51).

*I pay tribute to the unknown
authors of stories and
illustrations which could not be
traced to the proper source.
I apologize for any such instances.
If you recognize an uncited story,
please let me know and the
publisher and I will be sure to
acknowledge the author
in future printings*

Other Books by William E. Berg

for more information visit **www.bergbooks.com**

Show Me the Way to Go Home
Journey to the Promised Land

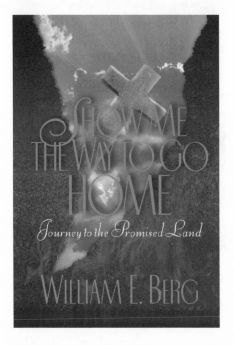

In this book, the author reminds us that the more heavenly-minded we are, the more practical our service will be in our Lord's work of healing and reconciliation in our broken world. He seeks to follow the Word of God Travel Service with Jesus Christ as Companion and Rescuer, and the Holy Sprit as Guide.

A Strange Thing Happened to Me on the Way to Retirement– I Never Arrived!

At the age of 90, the author in this book seeks to redefine retirement. He insists that there is no retirement policy in the Kingdom of God. Difficult choices and impairments of body and spirit in older age are recognized. The divine dimension of life as revealed in the Word of God is highlighted.

Prayer in the Name of Jesus
and Other Writings

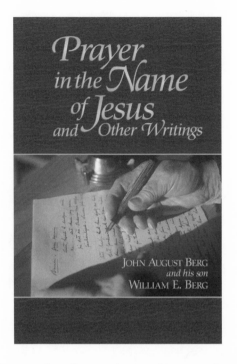

This book contains dramatic messages and stories from the lives of John A. Berg and his son, William E. Berg. John August Berg loved to walk. Walking and running with our Lord is the story of Amazing Grace and also the story of this book. Indeed, prayer is walking and talking with our Lord.

It's Okay Not to be Okay IF...

This is a book on the study of the *"Divine If's"*. The author wrote this book not least as a safeguard against the theology of cheap grace. Our God honors us with the priceless gifts of accountability and responsibility. He writes of the love of God which provides incentive and power to respond to His conditions.

Jesus
Final Authority on Marriage and Same-sex Unions

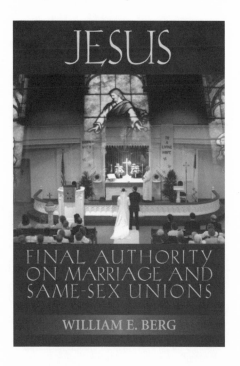

The title of this book may indicate to readers that its primary focus is on marriage and same-sex unions. Actually, the Word of God, reviewing Jesus as Final Authority, is the central message of the book. In the controversial issues of marriage and same-sex unions, we need to hear the Divine voice from heaven, "This is My beloved Son; listen to Him."

Study Notes

Study Notes

Study Notes

Study Notes

Study Notes

Study Notes

Study Notes

Study Notes

Study Notes

Study Notes

Study Notes